Walking on
Eggshells

Here, and not only here, there arises the problem of authority, of prescriptiveness. The entry of the Dictionary under **dictionary** *lays claim to nothing more than the recording of a word's origin, history and usage. And everyone will agree that the language must continue to change and develop as it always has done, is going to do regardless. Phrases like 'he has authored a dozen books' or 'the project is sound moneywise' cannot but cause irritation here and there, but they have evolved by the traditional processes of using noun as verb and tagging on a space-saving suffix.*

'What's in a Word?' from *The Amis Collection* – SIR KINGSLEY AMIS

The sound of the producers walking on eggshells was almost deafening.

'Walking on Eggshells' from *The Spectator* 20 May 2006
– SIMON HOGGART

Walking on Eggshells

Aspects of English usage

G E De Villiers

MACMILLAN

First published in 2007 by
Pan Macmillan South Africa
Private Bag X19
Northlands, 2116

www.panmacmillan.co.za

ISBN-13: 978-1-77010-062-6

ISBN-10: 1-77010-062-8

Typset in 9/14pt ITC Stone by Triple M Design & Advertising
Printed and bound in South Africa by
CTP Books, Cape

Contents

Introduction

Writing this book was like walking on eggshells! All this means is that I've had to be very careful about what I've had to say – and, even then, not everyone's going to agree with everything I've said. This is quite all right, simply because language usage, like fashion, is in a constant state of flux.

Thus, what was regarded as inviolable seventy, thirty, sometimes no more than ten years (years'?) ago, might no longer be seen as such. At times, this book is, therefore, as much about exceptions – and allowable alternatives – to rules, as about the rules themselves.

In fact, this is very much what has happened, and is still happening (oops, so nearly false ellipsis!), to the pronunciation of certain words. Take one like 'ate', for instance. Until not that long ago its pronunciation was fixed as 'et'; today, more and more are pronouncing it as 'eight', and this has now been given the stamp of approval by most dictionaries, listing it as an acceptable option to its earlier pronunciation. The same is true of words like 'harass' that (which?) can be pronounced either as 'harris' or 'ha-rass', or 'innovative', either as 'in-e-va-tive' or 'inno-ve-tive', or 'flaccid', as either 'flack-sid' or 'flas-sid'. In the same way, language usage is also not exempt from change, as the number of 'either ... ors' (or's?) in this book amply demonstrates (demonstrate?).

Now, there's nothing wrong with this, for that's how language develops and grows. What we must guard against, though, is inconsistency. In other words, if, for example, we spelt (or spelled) 'adviser' ('advisor' is also correct), with an 'e' at the beginning of a piece of writing, that form should be retained throughout. So, when it comes to matters of choice, consistency should always be the watchword.

This book is for those with an interest in language and its 'correct' use. I must stress that this is *not* a grammar book, although a little does inevitably feature – hopefully (is this word acceptable?), in an accessible and non-threatening way.

Furthermore, the book sets out (of course) to be informative but not, I hope, in deadly dull fashion, hence, among other things, the conversational tone and occasional lapse into colloquial expression.

Finally, I must stress that any errors in this book are either printer's gremlins or else were deliberately implanted in order to keep readers on their toes!

G E de Villiers

Abbreviations and Acronyms

It is one thing to abbreviate by contracting,
another by cutting off.

FRANCIS BACON (1561–1629)

Abbreviations and acronyms are useful, saving, as they do, both space and time, as well as – to an extent – ink! They also support ease of understanding. It's much simpler, for instance, to end a geometrical proof with **QED** – an acronym forever associated with that rascal Euclid, the scourge of generations of schoolchildren – than with its more ponderous Latin equivalent of **quod erat demonstrandum**. Likewise, **DNA** has, happily, become so much a part of today's vocabulary, that few remember – or bother to remember – that it derives from 'deoxyribonucleic acid'.

The word 'abbreviation' dates back to the 15th Century and refers, as we know, to the shortened form of a longer word or phrase (**Co.** = **Company**). An acronym, on the other hand, is of much more recent provenance, originating in the 1940s, and defines a word formed from the first letters of other words – or parts of them – and is sometimes pronounced as a word (**UN** = United Nations; **Unisa** = University of South Africa).

Acronyms and abbreviations are certainly the in-thing these days, for a very good reason. The ongoing pace of development in science, technology, commerce, industry, and so on, has resulted in the unprecedented emergence of, for instance, new words, phrases, technical terms, as well as names of organisations and institutions. Unfortunately, many of these coinages can best be described as 'jawbreakers', others as real 'mouthfuls'.

Thankfully, contractions are able to cut them down to size.

Let's instance an example or two: a while ago the UN set up an 'intergovernmental panel on climate change'; in a recent article reference was made, on at least ten occasions, to the workings of the panel. Had the name been used in full each time, readers might well have abandoned the article, doubtlessly suffering from a bad case of periphrastic burn-out! Instead, the user-friendly acronym, **IPCC**, was able to save the day. And what about this piece of good news: recently **MIT** launched an important initiative known as **OLPC**. Puzzled? All it means is that the **Massachusetts Institute of Technology** has initiated, through a non-profit organisation, a project dedicated to providing **one laptop per child**, presumably in the US. I prefer the acronyms – brief, crisp and concise.

On a lighter note: the late Ronnie Barker – the British comedian – in one of his personas, was the self-elected president of the **Society for the Pismounciation of Worms**; if ever a jawbreaker was in desperate need of an acronym, it's this one. What more obvious than **SPW**: it's agreeably mellifluous and impossible to pismounciate!

In the 1980s the number of abbreviations in the English language had just begun its ascent towards the half a million mark. And that's no exaggeration. However, this does not surprise me, for each day ushers in, not only the sun, but also – I'm convinced – at least a couple of newly minted abbreviations/acronyms as well!

The following acronyms and abbreviations were accessed by trolling through (mainly) the business sections of three Sunday, and two daily, newspapers and are arranged in no particular order.

Satawu (SA Transport and Allied Workers Union),
PTWU (Professional Transport Workers Union),
Popcru (Police and Prisons Civil Rights Union),
JSC (Judicial Service Commission),
Sacob (SA Chamber of Business),
M & A (mergers and acquisitions),
Santa (SA National Traders' Alliance),
Saica (SA Institute of Chartered Accountants),
Setas (Sector Education and Training Authorities),
NSDS (National Skills Development Strategy),
PFMA (Public Finance Management Act),
SSP (Sector Skills Plan),
LC (Labour Court),
NFVF (National Film and Video Foundation),
FSB (Financial Services Board),
BEE (Black Economic Empowerment)
Sapo (SA Port Operations),
IT (Information technology),
BITF (Black Information Technology Forum),
IDC (Industrial Development Corporation),
ETF (Exchange Traded Funds),
NEF (National Empowerment Fund),

dti (Department of Trade and Industry),

MIC (Mineworkers Investment Company),

CSI (Corporate Social Investment),

NUM (National Union of Mineworkers),

Icasa (Independent Communications Authority of SA),

LOA (Life Offices' Association),

PFA (Pension Fund Adjudicator),

ACI (Association of Collective Investments),

NSF (National Savings Fund),

DBSA (Development Bank of SA),

NUMSA (National Union of Metalworkers of SA),

PSC (Public Service Commission),

CGE (Commission of Gender Equality),

Scopa (Standing committee on public accounts),

NDPP (National Directorate of Public Prosecutions),

GM (genetically modified),

SACP (SA Communist Party),

RDP (Reconstruction and Development Programme),

SAARF (SA Advertising Research Foundation),

GEAR (Growth, Employment and Redistribution),

NEPAD (New Partnership of Africa's Development),

IEC (Independent Electoral Commission),

HRC (Human Rights Commission),

IMS (Integrated Manufacturing Strategy),

IRBA (Independent Regulatory Board of Auditors),

Asgisa (Accelerated and Shared Growth Initiative for SA),

TAC (Treatment Action Campaign),

Sascoc (SA Sports Confederation and Olympic
    Committee),
FPB (Film and Publication Board),
SADC (Southern African Development Community),
Nedlac (National Economic Development and
    Labour Council),
PHP (People's Housing Process),
NURCHA (National Urban Reconstruction and
    Housing Agency),
SATSA (Southern African Tourism Services
    Association),
NDA (National Development Agency),
MSEs (small and medium enterprises),
NAAMSA (National Association of Automobile
    Manufacturers of SA),
MIDP (Motor Industry Development Programme).

It makes you think, doesn't it?

Guidelines for the use of abbreviations and acronyms

As a general principle, avoid beginning a sentence with an abbreviation or acronym. And, on the *initial* use of either, especially of those less well known, write out in full, with the contraction in brackets: **Unique Selling Points (USP)**; thereafter, use only the contraction. Familiar abbreviations and acronyms need not be spelt out.

(i) A full stop is not used for abbreviations that start and end with the same letter as the word itself:
Mr, Mrs, Ms, Dr (Doctor), **Ltd, St** (Saint)

(ii) Use a full stop if the last letter of the abbreviation is not the same as that of the actual word:
Prof., approx., anon., b. (born), **p.** (page), **No./Nos.** (number/numbers), **Dr.** (Drive – as in **Munro Dr.**)

(iii) Do not use full stops for technical and scientific abbreviations:
km (kilometre), **cg** (centigram), **P** (Phosphorus), **As** (Arsenic), **mm** (millimetre), **cm** (centimetre), **m²** (square metre)

(iv) Use full stops for these Latin abbreviations:
   (a) **e.g.** (for example), **i.e.** (that is to say), **etc.** (and so on), **viz.** (namely, in other words), **a.m.** (before noon), **p.m.** (after noon), **ibid.** (used to refer to a previously mentioned work); and
   (b) for these, where the full stop is placed after the second contraction:
   et al. (and elsewhere), **ad lib.** (to speak in public without preparation), **pro tem.** (for the time being), **infra dig.** (beneath one's dignity). However, some dictionaries these days retain the full stop after **et al.**, but omit it after **ad lib**, **pro tem** and **infra dig**.

(v) Do not use full stops for upper case Latin abbreviations:
   AD (which comes before the date, i.e. AD**60**), BC (an English abbreviation: it comes after the date, i.e. **60** BC.) Both AD and BC are set in small capitals.
   Other examples: **NB, PS, RIP**

(vi) Abbreviations of university degrees do not take full stops:
   BA, BSc, MA, DPhil, PhD, LLB, MBA, FCP(SA)

(vii) Full stops after a person's initials may be used,

or omitted, according to personal preference:
J.C. Smuts, R.R.R. Dhlomo, J.P. Gore
or, and this is the modern tendency,
I P Shisana, A M Kearey, K G H Ngubane
(Once again, stick to your choice.)

(viii) Even if this is in conflict with the rule, use full
stops to avoid confusion:
f.o.r. (free on rail), not **for**; **f.o.b.** (free on board),
not **fob**

(ix) Acronyms, consisting of an initial capital,
followed by lower case letters, and
pronounced as words, are written without full
stops:
Cosatu (Congress of South African Trade Unions),
Unesco (United Nations Educational, Scientific and
Cultural Organisation), **Aids** – also **AIDS** (acquired
immune deficiency syndrome), **Eskom** (Electricity
Supply Kommissie)

(x) Acronyms made up of upper case letters,
which stand for what is referred to, do not
take full stops:
MPC (multimedia personal computer), **OCR**
(optical character recognition), **MPD** (multiple
personality disorder), **GDP** (gross domestic
product), **GMWA** (**Br**. General and Municipal

Workers Union), **FDA** (**US**, Food and Drug
Administration), **CAL** (Computer-assisted, or
computer-aided, learning), **HIV** (human immune
deficiency virus), **CIA**, **UK**, **BBC**, **ANC**, **VCR**, **DVD**

(xi) Some acronyms have become so familiar as
words, that they're written as such, i.e. with
small letters:
radar (**ra**dio **d**etection **a**nd **r**anging);
scuba (**s**elf-**c**ontained **u**nderwater **b**reathing
apparatus).

Apostrophes

(A) *Then it starts. And 's true's bob, fans,*
if you ever scheme showing people into they seats
is easy, let me tell you it's not. No ways.
I never had such a terrible time in my
whole entire life as that first night usheretting.

'Excuse the Patrons, Please' from *Darling Blossom* – JENNY HOBBS

(B) *'I'd've used Sellotape but Dee recommended this.*
I shouldn't've bothered one way or the other.'

With No One As Witness – ELIZABETH GEORGE

The words in bold in (A) and (B) are each speech contractions: **'s true's** of 'it is true as', **I'd've** of 'I would have' and **shouldn't've** of 'should not have'. The apostrophes have been used to indicate the omission of a letter, or letters. Let's take **'s true's** as an example. The first apostrophe takes the place of the **i**, **t** and **i** in **it is**; the second, of the **a** in **as**. This is particularly useful, because, if it hadn't been for the apostrophes, we'd have ended up with this **s true s**, and this **I d ve**, and this **shouldn t ve** – and then, where would we have been? Perhaps a little confused, even if only momentarily.

So, the apostrophe does perform the useful function of taking the place of omitted letters in contractions. Another example is the problematic **it's** – as in (A) – which is the shortened form of **it is**, often confused with its equally problematic sibling, the possessive **its** (no apostrophe). The latter refers to 'ownership' or 'belonging to', as in '**Its** paw was badly cut', but, thankfully, the prognosis is good, and '**It's** sure to heal within days.' A similar confusion frequently arises between **whose** (which indicates possession), as in '**Whose** pencil is this?'; and **who's**, meaning **who is**, as in '**Who's** talking?' Care should, therefore, be taken to distinguish between **its** and **it's**, and **whose** and **who's**. As with **its** and **whose**, these possessives also do *not* take the apostrophe: **ours**, **yours**, **hers**, **theirs**.

The word 'apostrophe' dates back to the 16th

Century, and comes from the Greek **apostrophus**, from **apostrephein**, meaning 'turn away'. (Does this imply the turning away of a letter, and then using an apostrophe in its place? I'm not sure, but it sounds reasonable!) According to *The Shorter Oxford English Dictionary on Historical Principles*, one of its earliest recorded usages in English is to be found in Shakespeare's *Love's Labour's Lost*, where one of the characters bemoans the fact that 'You find not the apostrophas ...' (iv.ii.123). Similarly, these days – often on signages in stores – we, too, 'find not the apostrophas', no matter how desperately we seek them out. Walk through any mall you like and you're sure to be affronted by horrors such as **mens outfitters** (men's), **womens change rooms** (women's) and **childrens department** (children's)! These are all well-worn examples, trotted out at regular intervals, to prove that the apostrophe is an endangered species. Is it really as bad as all this? I don't think so. Yes, it is, at times, abused, misused and forgotten, but generally editors of books, newspapers, journals, magazines, and so on, do respect the integrity of the apostrophe, insisting, with the possible exception of a few renegades, on correct usage.

So far, we have seen that the apostrophe performs a dual role: it signals the omission of a letter (or letters), and is used to indicate possession. There's one more thing to consider, and this we'll do by investigating the case of the **kwaito singers lyrics**.

The obvious question to ask is – the lyrics of how many kwaito singers? As it stands, the answer is, of course, not forthcoming. However, with an apostrophe before the **s** (**kwaito singer's lyrics**), we understand that the lyrics were written by one singer only, while an apostrophe after the **s** (**kwaito singers' lyrics**) tells us that more than one singer was involved. Thus, the position of the apostrophe allows us to differentiate between singular and plural usage.

An interesting sidelight is that, in Old English (i.e. the period up to about 1066), there was no apostrophe. Instead, **es** was used to indicate possession. As time moved on, however, the **e** was dropped and replaced by the apostrophe, thus **folioes** became **folio's**, **moones** became **moon's**, and so on.

And now we come to the rules for forming possessives, using the apostrophe:

Possessives of Nouns

(i) Add an **'s** to the singular form of the noun:
the dentist's drill
(i.e. the drill of the dentist; in many cases, you can test for the possessive by using the **of-method**)

(ii) For the plural form of nouns that end in **s**, add an apostrophe after the **s**:
the dentists' drills
(i.e. the drills of the dentists)

(iii) For the plural form of nouns that do not end in **s**, add an **'s**:
the children's bedroom
(i.e. the bedroom of the children)

(iv) An **'s** is added to a person's name for the possessive singular:
Blake's car
Dickens's house   *all singular*
Van der Poel's driveway

However, if a sort of 'hissing' or 'eez' sound results from adding an **'s** to the name of a person ending in **s**, then only an apostrophe is added after the **s**:

> **Francis' books**
> **Jesus' parables**   *all singular*
> **Moses' sayings**
> **Xerxes' enemies**

The difference between, say, **Dickens's house** and **Xerxes' enemies**, should now be clear.

(v) Add only an apostrophe after the plural form of names:
> **the Dickenses' house**
> **the Van der Merwes' children**   *all plural*
> **the Van Wyks' neighbours**

(vi) For joint ownership, add an **'s** to the final name in a series; for individual ownership add an **'s** to each name:
> **Adrian and Hilda's car** (joint ownership)
> **Adrian's and Hilda's clothes** (individual ownership)
> **Agatha and Agnes's businesses are flourishing** (joint ownership of the businesses)
> **Agatha's and Agnes's businesses are flourishing** (individual ownership of the businesses)

(vii) Your ear probably tells you that 'he is an enemy of her' is wrong, and that the possessive phrase '... of hers' should have been used instead. A clear distinction should, therefore, be drawn between:

He is an enemy of Monica (wrong).
AND **He is an enemy of Monica's** (right).

(viii) Notice, too, the difference between **That is a photograph of Archibald** and **That is a photograph of Archibald's**. The first refers to a picture, containing Archibald's likeness, whereas the second informs us that it belongs to him.

(ix) An **'s** is added to the noun in an appositional phrase and not to the name which precedes it. (The word 'apposition' refers to a phrase that follows a noun and has the same meaning as it.)
We must ask for Hamilton, the coach's, approval.
(Note that 'the coach' is in apposition to Hamilton, and it, not Hamilton, takes the apostrophe.)
BUT **We must ask for Hamilton's approval.**

(x) For the possessive form of the names of public holidays and other noteworthy days, follow the rule for nouns – an **'s** is usually added to the singular form; however, there are exceptions:
Father's Day, Mother's Day, St Patrick's Day, New Year's Day, St Valentine's Day
BUT **Parents' Day, April Fools' Day** or **April Fool's Day**
(the jury's out on this one!)

17

(xi) This is quite a difficult one: Do not use an apostrophe for words that are more informative than possessive:

a meeting of the boilermakers union (informative)

BUT **The boilermakers' strike was successful.** (possessive)

(xii) An **'s** is added to the final word in compound nouns, for both their singular and plural forms:

the Governor General's car (singular)
the Governors General's cars (plural)
the mother-in-law's suggestion (singular)
the mothers-in-law's suggestions (plural)

(xiii) Add an apostrophe to the possessive plural of dates:

the 1950s' style of dress

(xiv) If used possessively, add an apostrophe to words ending in **ce** or **ness**:

for goodness' sake
for appearance' sake

(xv) A small niggle – **Woolworths** does *not* take the apostrophe, unless used possessively:

We shop at Woolworths.

BUT **Woolworths' goods are of a high quality**.

(xvi) The following illustrates the idiomatic use of the apostrophe:

a day's wait – ten days' wait

a minute's time – ten minutes' time

an hour's interval – five hours' interval

one week's break – three weeks' break

a stone's throw, at his wits' end, a hair's breadth, to your heart's content, for old times' sake, for pity's sake, summer's end, water's edge, mind's eye

Possessives of Pronouns

(i) Add an **'s** to **else**, and not to the pronoun that precedes it:
someone else's file

(ii) However, if **else** is omitted, add an **'s** to the pronoun:
someone's book
another's faults

(iii) The word **other** takes an **'s** for the singular form, and an apostrophe after the **s** for its plural:
each other's cars (singular)
others' faults (plural)

Other uses of the apostrophe

(i) An apostrophe is used for the plural form of lower case letters:
spell with two m's and two t's
mind your p's and q's

(ii) An apostrophe is used to indicate that a number has been omitted:
back in '68, the '80s, '80s' attitudes
(yes, two apostrophes!)

(iii) Note that the following do not take apostrophes:
  dos and don'ts (apart from the contraction)
  no ifs, ands or buts
  pros and cons

Capitalisation

Mrs Dither of Dunkeld is anxious to form a Dunkeld Bus Unit. The objects of the club are Bus Watching, Bus Spotting, Bus Catching. Its chief aim is to find ways and means of avoiding Bus Waiting. The Dunkeld Bus Club, which will also be known as MI5A, will have reciprocity with MI5. There has already been an exchange of letters between Mrs Dither and Sir Percy Sillitoe, in which Mrs Dither undertakes to send food parcels if Sir Percy sends out three of his best men to investigate the mysterious disappearance of the Dunkeld Bus, which is now reported to be suffering from amnesia.

'Dunkeld Bus Club' from *The Passing Show* – JOEL MERVIS

The extract illustrates some of the uses of the capital letter. It is used for the initial letter in the first word of sentences (**Mrs**, **The**, **There**), for the first letter of designations (**Mrs**), titles (**Sir**), first names (**Percy**), surnames (**Dither**, **Sillitoe**) and place names (**Dunkeld**). Initial letters of important words in the names of organisations, etc. begin with capitals (**Dunkeld Bus Club**); the same may apply to words the writer wants to emphasise, or draw attention to, especially where the intention is to be humorous or ironic (**Bus Watching**, **Bus Spotting**, **Bus Catching**, **Bus Waiting**). Capitals are used for most acronyms (**MI5**); and, as the **Dunkeld Bus** is given the human attribute of suffering from amnesia, it is distinguished by initial capitals, as is the case for all proper nouns!

Capital letters are also known as upper case letters, and small letters as lower case letters. A question sometimes asked is how the distinction between them arose. First, we should bear in mind that our alphabet is largely based on the Latin model, which, to begin with, consisted of capital letters only. However, over a period of time, a lower case cursive form of writing was gradually developed, one of the reasons being the (happy) discovery that it is less laborious to write something cursively than in block capitals. (If you don't believe me, try it for yourself!) The result of all of this was that, by the 15th Century, an integrated system of upper case and lower case usage was pretty well established. (Capitals were kept on for the first letter of the first word of a sentence and as the initial letter of nouns.)

After this piece of potted history, let's turn our attention to the origin of the terms 'upper case' and 'lower case'. In the 17th Century – and until not that long ago! – typesetting was done by hand. Individual letters, made from a mixture of metals, were used to make up words. The letters – or 'types' – were kept in specially designed trays or cases. Each case consisted of a top, and a bottom, part. Capital letters were kept in the upper half of the case, small letters in the lower half. Hence capitals became associated with the upper case and small letters with the lower case. And that, in a nutshell, is how we arrived at these words.

The Uses of Capital Letters

(i) Use capitals for *specific*, but small letters for *general*, references:
a headmaster of a school (general)
the **Headmaster** of Ebenezer High **School** (specific)

(ii) Use small letters for titles of people or places, but capitalise when used with a proper noun:
His **uncle** was quite short.
His **Uncle Gilbert** is pretty tall.
There are two **universities** in the **province**.
There're desert areas in the North West **Province**.
He attended **Rhodes University**.

(iii) Capitals are necessary for:

names of people (**Jemima**), places (**Pofadder**), roads (**Harrow Road, Eloff Street, Oak Avenue, De Waal Drive – Road, Street**, etc. should not be written with a small letter), rivers (**Orange River** – write 'river' with a small letter if you wish, but I'd rather you didn't!), mountains (**Drakensberg Mountains**), buildings (**Johannesburg Art Gallery**).

names of historical periods (**Dark Ages**), historic

addresses (Macmillan's **Winds of Change** speech),
historical documents (**Magna Carta**), great
historic moments (**the Renaissance**), artistic and
architectural styles (**Impressionism, Romanesque**)
awards and prizes (**the Nobel Prize**).

names of organisations (**the Red Cross
Society**), institutions (**Rose Retirement Village**),
corporations (**South African Broadcasting
Corporation**), sporting events (**Commonwealth
Games**), government departments (**Department of
Trade and Industry**), political parties (**Democratic
Alliance**), alliances (the **Allies**).

names of days of the week (**Monday**), months of
the year (**June**), public holidays (**Family Day**).

names of groups (the **Second Years** were a bright
bunch), ethnic groupings (**Occidentals**).

'nicknames' (the **Sharks'** rugby team, the **Iron
Duke**).

names given to natural phenomena (**Hurricane
Katrina**), planets, constellations, etc. (**Mars**, the
Great Bear), natural features (**Okavango Swamp**),
geographic references (the **Tropics**).

names of churches (**Roman Catholic**) and *names
of adherents* (**Christians**); names given to the

Deity (**Jehovah**, **Allah**) and pronouns referring to the Deity (**They**, **Him**), but small letters for **who, whom, whose**; also capitals for names of religious orders (**Sisters of Mercy**).

names of animals, but small letters for the type (**Angora goat**, **Friesian cattle**).

abstract ideas or *inanimate objects* when personified (the call of **Nature**, **Beauty** in all her glory).

(iv) Use capitals for:
trade names (**Mrs Ball's Chutney**)
names of ships (*Queen Mary*)
aeroplane types (**Airbus**)
types of motor cars (**Kia**)
newspapers (*The Times*)
magazines (*Country Life*) and journals
(*National Geographic*)

(v) For the names of films, books, plays, musical compositions, operas and poems, use initial capitals for important words only:
The Squid and the Whale (film)
The Old Man and the Sea (book)
Androcles and the Lion (play)
Young Person's Guide to the Orchestra (musical composition)
A Night at the Chinese Opera (opera)
'Ode to a Nightingale' (poem)

(vi) Capitals are not used for adjectives, verbs and nouns derived from proper names, nor for the names given to scientific units, especially when the link with the original has become quite tenuous: **titanic struggle** (adjective), **to pasteurise milk** (verb), **put under a boycott** (noun); a **newton** (symbol N), **volt** (symbol V), **amp** (ampere, symbol A). The same is true for words like **quisling**, **macadamise**, **mackintosh**. Going against the grain is **Bunsen burner**, where the first letter is *always* capitalised, unlike, say, **wellington boots**, which is *usually* lower-cased. A point to bear in mind is that when the connection between 'word' and 'name' is still reasonably close, as in **Freudian slip**, an initial capital is required. The word, **Judas** – meaning traitor or betrayer – also begins with a capital , this because of its specific reference to the biblical character; if, on the other hand, the allusion is to a **judas**, i.e. a peephole in a door, it is written with a small letter.

(vii) Capitals are not used in the names of areas of study, knowledge or interest, unless they refer to particular subjects:
He failed History at school.

BUT **The town has a fascinating history.**
She dropped Geography after Grade Eight.
BUT **She knows little about the geography of the place.**
He majored in Economics at university.
BUT **He has much to learn about the economics of business.**

(viii) **North, South, East, West**: used adjectivally, these take an initial capital, when part of a name: **North Pole, South Africa, East Timor, West Indies**; as an adverb, small letters are used: they flew **north** (**south/east/west**); as adjectives, **northern, southern, eastern, western** are written in the lower case: **The lighthouse ... situated on the northern/ southern/eastern/western side of the bay** – however, when they form part of a name, capitals are used: **Northern Ireland, Southern Cross, Eastern Cape, Western Isles**; but, write **southern Africa** (lower case **s**) as here it does not function as part of a name, but instead refers to a region with no defined boundaries: **They travelled across southern Africa**. For directional abbreviations, use the upper case: **NE** (north-east), **SSW** (south-south-west).

(ix) A capital follows:
- a **full stop**: 'You're being difficult. Go on like this and you'll soon be in trouble.'
- an **exclamation mark**, when it ends a full sentence: 'What a load of nonsense! In fact, you're completely out of order.'; but not after a word or phrase: 'Oh dear! that's really got me thinking.'
- a **question mark**: 'Why are you asking me that again? That's about the third time you've asked me the same thing.'
- a **colon**, but only after a full sentence: 'This is what I want to know: Where did you go last night?' No capital is used if a phrase, or series of phrases, follows: 'This is what I asked for: two loaves of bread and half a dozen eggs.'

(x) All of the examples in (ix) are written in direct speech; note that in each instance the first letter of the first word is a capital. The same applies to the dialogue in a play, where a capital follows the name of the speaker:
Hamlet: Now, mother, what's the matter?

In general, too, the first letter of each line of poetry, or song, is capitalised:

Tyger! Tyger! burning bright
In the forests of the night,
What immortal hand or eye
Could frame they fearful symmetry?

(xi) For botanical references, use a small letter for the *general* but a capital for the *particular*:
One variety of **violet** (general) is known as **Viola odorata** (specific)

The same applies to ornithological terms:
Two species of **duck** (general) are the **Yellowbilled Duck** and the **African Black Duck** (particular).

(xii) Titles and the definite article. Unless it forms a part of the title, the definite article must be written roman lower case:
The Star BUT the *Daily Mirror*
The Daily Telegraph BUT the *International Herald Tribune*
The Sunday Independent BUT the *Sunday Times*

(xiii) Surnames with particles. When a surname with a particle, e.g. **van**, **van der**, **de**, **le**, **de la**, etc., is preceded by the person's initial/s or name/s the particle is lower case:
N D van der Merwe, Jan le Roux
If the surname is used on its own, the particle begins with a capital:
De la Rey, Van Poggenpoel
*(Note that the second particle, i.e. **la**, is always lower case.)*

If the surname (without initials or first names) is preceded by a designation, the particle may either be lower or upper case – it's up to you; thus,

Rev. Dr van der Tromp *OR* **Rev. Dr Van der Tromp**
Prof. van Rooyen *OR* **Prof. Van Rooyen**

'Correcting'
Common 'Errors'*

*Speech is the primary reality, loose, inexact,
crammed with solecisms, its grammar atrocious,
but it is what human communication is all about.*

'The Times as Guardian' from *Homage to Qwert Yuiop* – ANTHONY BURGESS

*The inverted commas are essential!

When it comes to grammatical usage, it's important to emphasise that there's often a world of difference between the written and spoken word. In informal speech, such as ordinary conversation, neither we, nor, for that matter, characters in fiction, are obliged to stick to the rules. Therefore, if we say 'It's them' instead of 'It's they', or 'They picked his pocket, without him even being aware of it' instead of '... without his even being aware of it', that's fine.

However, is it all right to do the same thing in a more formal piece of writing, such as a business report, or an article for a technical journal, or even in the indirect speech connectives in a novel or short story? My immediate response would be to say 'No, it's not OK'. On the other hand, I hesitate to do so. The reason? Well, because these days, usage seems to dictate what is acceptable and unacceptable. Let's take an example: it was once deemed a capital offence to end a sentence with a preposition. Not so, any more. The present attitude is that, if it doesn't send a painful shock through your body, then, by all means, go ahead and terminate your sentences with that inoffensive little part of speech; after all, nobody is going to get hurt, if that's the route you choose to take!

But, despite all of this, I still believe that we should reject the idea of 'anything goes'. Yes, some of the rules of grammar have reached their sell-by date, but certainly not all of them. Therefore, I intend to devote this section to highlighting the 'correct' version of some of the more common grammatical 'errors' we quite often come across in print. Before doing so, though, I intend to have a quick look at a little bit of grammar, of the variety we did at school, to assist in our getting to grips with 'incorrect' usage. If you still remember all of this, then skip what's to follow; if not, I promise the journey will be painless!

A little bit of Grammar

Parts of Speech

1. **Noun**: is a naming word. There are four types –

   Proper: John, Durban; **Common**: desk, roof; **Abstract**: beauty, conscience; **Collective**: flock, herd.

2. **Pronoun**: stands in place of a noun – **I**, **we**, **me**, **us**, **you**, **he**, **she**, **it**, **they**, **him**, **her**, **them**.

3. **Verb**: traditionally defined as a 'doing' word; e.g. **talk**, **sing, sniff, hate, despair, laugh, flinch, run, mutter**; very importantly, there is also what is known as the verb 'to be', i.e. **is**, **are**, **was**, **were**, **am**.

4. **Auxiliary Verbs**: are 'helping' verbs e.g. **had** spoken, **should have** spoken, **should have been** speaking.

5. **Adjective**: **qualifies** (describes) a noun – it answers the question *which*? before a noun, e.g. the **strong** woman, the **long** silence.

6. **Adverb**: it usually ends in **ly**, and **modifies** (tells us something more about) a **verb**, e.g. He ran **slowly** (modifies the verb 'ran'); or an **adjective**, e.g. She is a **very** strong woman (modifies the adjective 'strong'); and can sometimes even modify another **adverb**, e.g. He spoke **extremely** quickly (modifies the adverb 'quickly').

7. **Preposition**: in 'the computer **on** the desk', the word 'on' is a preposition for three reasons: it comes before a noun ('desk'), it introduces a phrase ('on the desk') and it shows the relationship between two words (i.e. where the computer is in relation to the desk – **on**, not 'beside', 'below' or 'beneath'.) All prepositions function in the same way. Other examples are: **in**, **to**, **for**, **with**, **after**.

8. **Conjunction**: is a 'joining' word. There are two types:

   Subordinate conjunctions, e.g. I know **where** he stays – 'where' joins 'I know' to 'he stays'. Other examples: **if**, **unless**, **though**, **when**, **where**, **who**, **that**.

   Co-ordinate conjunctions: there are only four of them: **and**, **but**, **or**, **nor**, e.g. He ignored the traffic **and** [he] just ambled across the road. (A subordinate conjunction introduces a lesser important part of the sentence, while a co-ordinate conjunction introduces a part of the sentence that is as important as the main part.)

9. **Interjection**: words like **Alas**! **Oh**!

10. **Articles**: **the** is called the **definite article**, while **a** and **an** are **indefinite articles**.

Subject, Object, Complement (of a verb)

Subject and Object

Sophia hurled the javelin.

Subject: Test for the subject by asking who? or what? *before* the verb, i.e. **who**? or **what**? hurled the javelin? The answer is 'Sophia', therefore Sophia is the subject of the verb 'hurled'.

Object: In the same sentence, test for the object by asking the same questions *after* the verb, i.e. Sophia hurled **who**? or **what**? The answer is 'the javelin', therefore it is the object of the verb 'hurled'. An object may also be governed by a preposition; apply the same test **after** a preposition:

He spoke to me.

Ask who? or what? *after* the preposition i.e. He spoke to **who(m)**? or **what**? The answer is 'me', therefore it is the object of the preposition 'to'.

(Notice, then, that the subject of a verb is always a noun or pronoun, as is the object of a verb or preposition. There are also noun phrases and clauses, which, however, are not our immediate concern.)

Complement

Janice is a mud wrestler.

Complement: In this sentence the verb 'is', as you'll recall, is a part of the verb 'to be'. The noun that follows the verb 'to be' is known as the complement, as it completes the incomplete part of the sentence, i.e. **Janice is**, is incomplete on its own. Test for the complement by asking who? or what? *after* the verb 'to be': Janice is **who?** or **what**? The answer is 'a mud wrestler', which is, therefore, the complement of the verb 'is'.

Finite and Non-finite Verbs

Finite verb: is a verb that takes a subject. Thus, in the above sentences, both **hurled** and **is** are finite verbs, as both have subjects.

Non-finite verb: is a verb that has no subject, e.g. **told a story.** As the verb **told** has no subject, it is non-finite.

Phrase and Clause

Phrase: is a group of words *without* a finite verb; furthermore, the phrase does not make sense on its own, e.g. **in the evening, singing in the bath, late for lunch.**

Clause: is a group of words that *contains* a finite verb, e.g. **Herbert likes playing tiddlywinks; although Herbert likes playing tiddlywinks; Spiderman and Superman are**. (Notice that a clause does not necessarily have to make sense on its own.)

Main, Co-ordinate and Subordinate Clauses

A **main clause** is one introduced by the subject of a verb, a **co-ordinate clause** by a co-ordinate conjunction, and a **subordinate clause** by a subordinate conjunction: **The accused shouted** (main clause – introduced by the subject 'The accused') **and hurled abuse** (co-ordinate clause – introduced by co-ordinate conjunction 'and') **when he was sentenced** (subordinate clause – introduced by subordinate conjunction 'when').

With all of the above in mind, we should now be sufficiently well equipped to tackle some of the more common 'errors' that we sometimes encounter in our language.

(i) Misrelated Participle

A participle is a word that 'participates' in two parts of speech, i.e. it is, at one and the same time, a verb and a 'sort' of adjective. A misrelated participle is when, in a sentence, the participle relates (i.e. refers) to an incorrect subject:

> **Strolling** down the lane, the **street-lights**
> glowed brightly.

Strolling is a participle, being both a verb (the act of doing something) and an adjective (as it qualifies or describes the noun 'street-lights'). This is clearly incorrect, as it is highly improbable that the street-lights were strolling. To correct the sentence, insert a suitable subject after the comma:

> **Strolling** down the lane, **Helga** became aware of
> the brightly glowing street-lights.

Participles end in either *ing*, *en* or *ed*, or are introduced by *having* or *being* followed by a verb, e.g. *having heard*, *being interested*. They can qualify a single word (The **frightened** dog), or, as we've seen, introduce a phrase.

(ii) Gerunds incorrectly qualified

Like the participle, the gerund ends in **ing**. It also participates in two parts of speech i.e. it is a verb and a 'sort' of noun. It can either be the subject of a verb, or the object of a verb or preposition:

> **Reading** is pleasant. (subject of verb 'is')
> Helga enjoys **skating**. (object of verb 'enjoys')
> On **being** nominated for the award ... (object of
> preposition 'on')

As the gerund has a 'noun' element to it, it must be qualified by an adjective. A mistake often made is to use a

43

pronoun to qualify the gerund, as in this sentence:

> On **him being** nominated for the award, he
> immediately started organising a celebratory
> party.

The (possessive) adjective 'his' should have been used in place of the pronoun 'him' i.e. On **his being** nominated ... Therefore, in these instances, change **I/me** to **my**, **we/us** to **our**, **you** to **your**, **he/him** to **his**, **she** to **her**, **they/ them** to **their**. (Replace 'him' in the above sentence, with each of these alternatives, to test for incorrect and correct usage.)

(iii) Number

We sometimes come across sentences where the number of a verb does not agree with the number of its subject, i.e. where a singular verb is used with a plural subject and vice versa. Here, now, are the rules for correct usage:

> (a) Use a singular verb when two nouns refer
> to one person or thing:
>
> The **wife and mother** *is* totally unreliable.
> (one person)
>
> **Whiskey and soda** *is* a pleasant drink.
> (one drink)
>
> If, however, the definite article is inserted
> before the second noun, a plural verb is
> needed:

The **wife and the mother** *are* ... (two separate people)
The **whiskey and the soda** *are* on the table.
(two separate drinks)

(b) **With**-phrases and **as well as**-phrases. Here the number of the verb agrees with the first noun:
The **mother** with her children *was strolling* in the park.
The **children** as well as their mother *were strolling* in the park.

(c) **Not only ... but also**-phrases and **Either ... or, Neither ... nor**. For these, the verb agrees with the number of the last noun:
Not only the singer but also many of her **fans** *were* there.
Neither her fans nor the **singer** *was delayed*.

(d) If the word **number** is preceded by an indefinite article, the verb is usually plural, but singular for the definite article:
A small **number** of spectators *were* present.
The small **number** of spectators *was* unusual.

(e) **Collective nouns**: use a singular verb when the collective noun refers to a group *as a*

whole, but a plural verb when the reference
is to *individuals* in the group:
The **crew** *is* said to be dissatisfied.
The mutinous **crew** *are* to be tried **separately**.

(f) **No one** (no hyphen), **anybody**, **everyone**,
anyone, **everybody** – all take singular verbs
and pronouns:
No one *was* going to own up.
Everyone *was* asked to take off **his** blazer.
(A common mistake is to replace the singular
possessive with a plural, i.e. **their blazer**, in order
to accommodate both genders. One could get away
with 'his/her', but this is clumsy, so rather recast
the sentence:
Both **boys and girls** *were* asked to take off
their blazer.)

(g) **None**: this is one of those problematic
words. For many years, the rule was
unequivocal: 'none' must always be
followed by a singular verb, as in a sentence
such as this one:
None of the twenty boys at those five schools
was accused of stealing the peaches.

However, these days, it can either be singular or

plural, and this determines the number of the verb to follow:

None of the **fruit** *is* rotten.

None of the **peaches** *are* fresh.

(Usually, if the noun which follows 'none' is plural ('peaches'), use a plural verb, if not, stick with the singular form.)

(h) Nouns like these always take singular verbs:
measles, **mumps**, **mathematics**, **news**.

(i) **Data**: its singular form is 'datum', but this is rarely used any more; instead, 'data' is preferred for both the singular and plural forms. However, there's a further twist in the plot – it is becoming more and more acceptable to use the singular verb for both cases, thus:

Most of the **data** *is* available.

The **data** *was* accessed over a period of time.

(I prefer this, although 'were' would not have been incorrect.)

(j) **Media**: when referring to a group as a whole, use the singular form, but the plural when referring to individuals in the group:

The **media** *is* usually objective in its reporting.

> After the meeting, the **media** *were* seen
> dashing for their cars.

(k) Depending on context, words ending in **ics**
   can be either singular or plural:
   Tactics *is* important in sport.
   Her **tactics** *were* questionable.

(Try similar structures with, say, 'politics'.)

(iv) Is/Are

It is sometimes difficult to decide, in sentences such as the following ones, whether to use the singular or plural form of the verb. The secret is to remember that the verb must always agree with the number of its subject, even if this, perhaps, results in the sentence sounding a bit odd!

The reason for the destruction is the heavy winds.
(Correct – here the subject, 'The reason [for the destruction]' is singular, therefore the singular verb 'is' must be used; please note that 'the heavy winds' is *not* the subject.)

The heavy winds are the reason for the destruction.
(Correct – the subject 'The heavy winds' is plural, therefore the plural verb 'are' must be used.)

(v) Was/Were

The word mood refers to the three forms of the

verb, namely, the indicative, the imperative, and the **subjunctive**. The function of the latter is to express a **condition**, a **wish**, **something imagined**, and so on. Our concern is to decide when to use 'was' and 'were' in the subjunctive. For instance, it is not easy to decide between 'If I **were** you' and 'If I **was** you'. As a general rule, though, use 'were' for **possibility**, but 'was' for **fact**.

Let me explain: 'If he **were** to ask, tell him I'm not here' – correct, as there's only a **possibility** that he'll ask; 'He was told to find out if it **was** (not **were**) allowable" – correct, he was asked to determine a **fact**, i.e. whether it would be allowed or not. You'll find that these structures normally take 'were': '**If I ... were; as if ... were; as though ... were**. (On the other hand, as we've seen, if it ... takes **was**.) Interestingly, 'were' used to be the preferred word – not 'was' – but these days writers seem to use them interchangeably. So, I suppose, can all of us, as long as we use the one or the other consistently. However, these illustrate 'correct' usage:

> If I **were** that bad, why stick with me?
> (possibility)
> He spoke, as if he **were** still half asleep.
> (possibility)
> She groaned, as though she **were** in the utmost
> agony. (possibility)
> If it **was** not clear to you, you should have said
> so. (fact)

> He would intervene, if it **was** proved they were in
> the wrong. (fact)

In these sentences, though, if the odd 'were' **was** (**were**?) to be changed to 'was', and vice versa, I wouldn't quibble! As you've probably realised by now, this is quite a tricky one.

(vi) Pronouns: Correct and Incorrect usage

These pronouns are used only as the SUBJECT or COMPLEMENT of a **verb**: **I**, **we**, **he**, **she**, **they**; these only as the OBJECT of a **verb** or **preposition**: **me**, **us**, **him**, **her**, **them**. (The pronoun **you** is used as either a subject or object.) These sentences illustrate correct usage:

> **I** spoke to **him**.

(**I** is correct as it is the subject of the verb 'spoke'; **him** is also correct as it is the object of the preposition '**to**'.)

> There is little difference in height between **you**
> and **me**.

(**me** is correct as it is the object of the preposition 'between'; and, as **you** may either be a subject or object, its use here as an object is correct.)

These sentences are **grammatically** incorrect:

> It is **them**.

> (**them** should be replaced by **they** as the complement
> of 'is' is required.)

It's **me**.

(**me** should be replaced by **I** as the complement of 'is' is required.)

Let you and **I** go.

(**I** should be replaced by **me** as the object of the verb 'let' is required.)

You and **me** should not have done that.

(**me** should be **I** as the subject of the verb 'should [not] have done' is required.)

On behalf of my wife and **I**, I'd like to thank you for being here tonight.

(This is a mistake speakers often make: **I** should, of course, be **me** as the object of the preposition 'of' is required.)

He is younger than **me**.

(What we are actually saying here is 'He is younger than **I** [am]'; in other words, [am] is not stated but is understood – therefore, **me** is wrong, as the subject, **I**, of the understood verb [am], is required.)

At this point, I must revert to what I said at the beginning of this section, namely, that usage determines what is correct and what is not. Therefore, in conversation with others, or in the dialogue in books, on stage, or on screen, it is perfectly acceptable to say 'It is me' or 'I am much younger than him'; however, in more formal usage, it is, perhaps, preferable to be grammatically correct.

(vii) Who/Whom

Who is used as the SUBJECT of a **verb**, **whom** as the OBJECT of a **verb** or a **preposition**. In these sentences **who** and **whom** are used correctly:

> **Who** is that?

(Correct: **Who** is the subject of the verb 'is'.)

> To **whom** were you speaking?

(Correct: **whom** is the object of the preposition 'to'.)

> That is the man **whom** he saw.

(Correct: although positioned before it, **whom** is the object of the verb 'saw'.)

The second sentence above is often wrongly given as:

> **Who** were you speaking **to**?

(It is no longer regarded as grammatically incorrect to end a sentence with a preposition. However, in this sentence, **who** should be replaced by **whom** as it is the object of the preposition 'to' – despite its coming at the end of the sentence. Grammatically, therefore, the sentence should read **To whom were you speaking?**)

I must again emphasise that certain structures may be used in informal speech, as in the above sentence, but with caution in more conventional forms of writing.

(viii) That/Which

When to use 'that' and when to use 'which' requires an understanding of what is meant by an adjectival clause. Simply, it's a clause (remember? – a group of words with a finite verb), which acts as an adjective, i.e. it qualifies a noun. The adjectival clause is introduced by one of the following subordinate conjunctions, coming immediately after the noun the clause qualifies: **who**, **whom**, **whose**, **which**, **that**, **when**, **where**, e.g.

> The place, **where she boards**, has been sold.
> (**where she boards** is an adjectival clause qualifying
> the noun 'place'.)

With this in mind, we can now move on to the difference in use between 'that' and 'which': the first introduces **a defining (or restrictive) adjectival clause**, the other a **non-defining (or non-restrictive) adjectival clause**. (See also under Punctuation.) **A defining clause** is *never* enclosed within commas, and contains essential information, which cannot be left out of the sentence without affecting its meaning; a **non-defining clause** is *always* enclosed within commas, and merely describes or comments on the noun it qualifies – furthermore, if left out, the meaning of the sentence will not be materially affected. These illustrate the point:

> The road **that hugs the coastline** is the one you
> want.
> (The adjectival clause contains essential information,
> for it identifies the particular road being sought
> – therefore, use **that** and omit commas.)
> The road, **which is pretty scenic**, hugs the
> coastline.

(The adjectival clause is merely descriptive, and can be left out, as it adds little more to the sentence than an inessential comment – therefore, use **which** and insert commas.)

Here are two more examples:

> The documents **that require your immediate attention** are in the blue folder.

(A defining clause; without it, essential information about the 'documents' would be missing.)

> The documents, **which were posted last week**, arrived this morning.

(A non-defining clause: it contains non-essential information, as it does no more than describe the 'documents'.)

(ix) Owing to/Due to

Much like the adjectival clause in (viii) above, **due to** functions adjectivally and must, therefore, qualify a noun. **Owing to**, on the other hand, acts very much like a participle, introducing a 'sort' of participial phrase (refer back to Misrelated Participle). If this is too much, forget about it: instead, use **owing to** when it can be replaced by 'as a result of' or 'because of' and, **due to**, in the sense of 'caused by':

> **Owing to matters beyond our control, we were not able to arrive on time.**

(Correct: **owing to = because of**)

> **The crash was undoubtedly due to poor**
> **visibility.**

(Correct: **due to = caused by**)

(x) The Pluperfect Tense

This refers to two actions in the past, the one being completed before the next begins. For the **pluperfect** – or the **past perfect tense**, as it is also known – the auxiliary verb 'had' must be attached to the past participle (a word ending in **ed** or **en**) in the **first action**. This is the mistake often made:

> **After she washed her clothes, she hung them**
> **out to dry.**

To correct, insert 'had' before the past participle 'washed':

> **After she had washed her clothes, she hung**
> **them out to dry.**

(xi) Split Infinitive

An infinitive is when 'to' is followed by a verb, e.g. **to drink**, **to go**, **to sing**. A split infinitive is when the infinitive is 'split' by another word being inserted between 'to' and the verb, e.g. **to really know**, **to fully realise**. To correct a sentence containing a split infinitive, recast the sentence so that 'to' immediately precedes the verb:

He used **to frequently say** … (Wrong)

He frequently used **to say** … (Right)

The split infinitive is no longer regarded as a major error. Therefore, keep it, if the sentence sounds all right; if not, get rid of it! In a letter to his publisher, Raymond Chandler, famous writer of PI crime stories, had this to say on the matter: 'When I split an infinitive, god damn it, I split it so it stays split.'

(xii) One/You

If you start by using **one** in a piece of writing, no matter how short or long, use it throughout, i.e. don't switch to **you** and vice versa:

One must be careful to see that **you** don't
overspend.

(Incorrect: replace **you** with **one** to ensure consistency of usage.)

(xiii) Each other/One another

Each other refers to two people, animals, etc., while **one another** refers to more than two:

The **two boys** shouted at **each other**.

The **four of them** kept interrupting **one another**.

These days, this distinction is no longer taken that seriously; however, if you are going to use them interchangeably, see that you keep to one or the other throughout.

(xiv) Like and As/As if

Simply, use **like** if it is followed by a phrase, but **as/as if**, if followed by a clause:

> **Do not behave like I do.**
>   (Incorrect: 'like' is followed by the clause 'I do';
>   change 'like' to 'as'.)

> **He drinks like a fish.**
>   (Correct: 'like' is followed by the phrase 'a fish'.)

> **She worked as if her life depended on it**.
>   (Correct: 'as if' is followed by a clause.)

It is, of course, all right to use 'like' in colloquial speech, as in 'It looks like it is going to rain'; it is also acceptable, if used in a slogan *'The Star* tells it like it is.'

(xv) False Ellipsis

Ellipsis is when a word/words in a sentence is/are omitted but understood:

> **He entered the room and ˄ sat down.**
>   (Although omitted, it is understood that 'he' follows
>   'and', i.e. ... and [he] sat down.)

False ellipsis is when the understood word/words is/are incorrect:

Few ever have ˄ **or can accept defeat**.

As it stands, the understood word is incorrect, i.e.

Few ever have [accept] or can accept defeat.

To correct, insert the correct word:

Few ever have accepted or can accept defeat.

Here's another example of false ellipsis:

She is as talented ˄, **if not more talented than,**
you.

(Wrong, as 'than' is understood after 'talented'; to
correct, insert 'as' after 'talented'.)

(xvi) Ambiguity

This refers to a statement that can have more than one
meaning. It should be avoided at all costs, as it can result
in unnecessary misinformation. This sentence is pretty
obviously ambiguous:

She informed her she was invited to the party.

(Who was invited? – the speaker or the one spoken to?)

Helga informed Mathilda that she, Mathilda,
was invited to the party.

(A bit cumbersome, but at least the ambiguity has been
removed.)

Especial care should be taken to place 'only' in its
correct position in the sentence, to avoid jeopardising the
intended meaning:

Only Terence wore a jacket and tie to work.

(i.e. Terence and no one else.)

Terence wore only a jacket and tie to work.

(i.e. that's all he wore – no trousers, shoes, etc.)

Terence wore a jacket and tie to work only.

(i.e. to nowhere else but work.)

The trick is, of course, to use 'only' next to the word it refers to.

(xvii) Mixed Metaphor

A metaphor is a figure of speech in which a suggested comparison is made between two unlike things:

He was a tiger in the ring.

(This is an indirect comparison between a boxer and a tiger and is, therefore, a metaphor.)

A **mixed metaphor** is when two mutually exclusive or contradictory metaphors are used in a single image:

He was a real tiger in business and thus had little problem in bulldozing his way to the top.

(This is a mixed metaphor as the businessman is, at one and the same time, said to be a tiger and a bulldozer! To correct the image, sustain one or other of the comparisons:

> **He was a real tiger in business and thus had**
> **little problem in clawing his way to the top**.

Clearly 'tiger' and 'clawing' belong together, and, thus,
the metaphor is no longer mixed.)

The film mogul, Sam Goldwyn, was renowned for mixing
his metaphors; on one occasion, he apparently came up
with this gem:

> **Every director bites the hand that lays the**
> **golden egg.**

Correct Usage

(A) ' – and as she grew up, I would have her instructed in geometry, that she might know something of the contagious countries ... and likewise that she might reprehend the true meaning of what she is saying.'

(B) 'He is the very pine-apple of politeness.'

(C) 'She's as headstrong as an allegory on the banks of the Nile.'

The quotations contain examples of malapropisms. The word is named after Mrs Malaprop, a character in Richard Sheridan's play, *The Rivals* (1775), who often used an incorrect word in place of another that sounded like it; this was clearly done to achieve a humorous effect. Thus, in (A) Mrs Malaprop has confused 'geometry' with 'geography', 'contagious' with 'contiguous' and, 'reprehend' with 'apprehend'. By 'pine-apple' in (B) she meant 'pinnacle' and, in (C), 'allegory', should, of course, be 'alligator'.

Confusables, though normally not as extreme as those perpetrated by Mrs Malaprop, are the subject of this section, together with a look at other words sometimes misused – and this, to appropriate a phrase uttered by Groucho Marx in the film *Cocoa-Nuts*, is no 'poultry matter'!

a/an

If a word begins with a sounded 'h' use **a**, e.g. **a hostel** but if the 'h' is not sounded use **an**, e.g. **an hour**. For words with an initial vowel, use **an**, e.g. **an eggplant**. Use **a** for words beginning with a consonant, e.g. **a song**, and with a vowel pronounced like a consonant, e.g. **a unicorn**.

acknowledgement/acknowledgment

I prefer the first, although **acknowledgment** is not wrong.

adviser/advisor

Both are correct, but I prefer **adviser**.

affect/effect

affect means

- to have an influence on: **Smoking has affected his throat**.
- to arouse feelings of sadness or sympathy: **The news of his accident deeply affected us**.

effect means

- to result in something: **The medicine had a positive effect on him**.
- to create an impression: **The play had a profound effect on me**.
- the state of bringing something about: **The plan will come into effect at midnight**.

Two in one: **Although the news had a devastating effect on Marmaduke, it did not really affect anyone else**.

The word **effects** refers to one's belongings: **his personal effects**.

afflict/inflict

afflict: to cause pain or trouble to someone/something

inflict: to cause something (usually unpleasant) to happen to somebody

Two in one: **He is afflicted with gout, no doubt inflicted on him by his passion for red wine.**

aggravate/irritate

In colloquial speech **aggravate** has come to have the same meaning as **irritate**, i.e. to make someone angry or annoyed. However, to the purist, the correct meaning of aggravate is to make a bad situation even worse: **He aggravated** (made worse) **the injury to his leg by starting to jog too soon.**

ago

The mistake is often made of having **since** follow the word 'ago', instead of **that** or **when: It is three years ago that** (not 'since') **I last saw him.**

all ready/already

Two in one: **Are you all ready** (i.e. fully prepared) **to go, because it is already** (i.e. by this time) **very late?**

all together/altogether

all together: all in one group, or on the same occasion

altogether: entirely; completely; on the whole

Two in one: **Let us, all together** (all of us on this occasion) **make it known that we are not altogether** (entirely) **happy with the decision.**

allusion/illusion

allusion: to make an indirect reference to something, e.g. **Any allusion** (reference) **to poverty upsets him.**

illusion: refers to a false idea, or piece of deception, e.g. **It's a complete illusion** (false idea) **to believe that life is a bed of roses**.

a lot

Can only be written as two words; *never* as one word.

alternate/alternative

alternate: refers to things happening one after the other, e.g. **a pattern of alternate red and white tiles**; also refers to 'every second', e.g. **on alternate months**, i.e. January, March, May, etc. (i.e. every second month).

alternative: something that can be got in place of something else, e.g. **to find an alternative place to stay**; it can also refer to one of two possibilities, e.g. **One of the alternatives is not to leave./There is no other alternative.**

ambiance/ambience

Both spellings are correct.

among/amongst
Use interchangeably, although the second is generally regarded as a little old-fashioned.

amount/number
Both refer to quantity. Use 'amount' when it relates to mass (**a large amount of water**), and 'number' when it refers to separate units, objects or individuals (**a large number of people**).

annual/perennial
annual: happening once a year (**an annual event**)

perennial: lasting for a number of, or many, years; lasting throughout the year (**a perennial issue**).

any one/anyone
any one: any *single* person, thing or object, e.g. **Any one of those answers is acceptable** (i.e. any single one).

anyone: *in general*, any person or persons, e.g. **Anyone is allowed to attend**.

around/round
Apart from a few instances, these may be used interchangeably, though the preference these days is for 'round' (but in the US for 'around'!) Always use

'around', though, in the sense of 'more or less', e.g.
There will be around twenty people present (but
'about' is just as good). Use 'round' in expressions
which have become almost idiomatic: **round
something down/off/up**, or **to round on** (verbally
attack) **a person**.

assure/ensure/insure

assure: to say something positively and confidently; to
guarantee (**I assure you that ...**)

ensure: to make something certain (**I will ensure that ...**)

insure: to safeguard your property by taking out an
insurance policy which will pay out in the event of
theft or loss (**to insure one's possessions against
theft**). Apart from the previous sense, **insure** is
sometimes used interchangeable with **ensure** – but,
remember, you can't **ensure** your house, only **insure** it!

astrology/astronomy

astrology: the study of the movement of stars and
planets as a means of interpreting their influence on
the lives of people, i.e. foretelling their future

astronomy: the scientific study of the universe, i.e.
stars, planets, galaxies, etc.

awhile/a while

awhile: for a **short** time; it is used as an **adverb**, e.g. **He rested awhile**.

a while: for a period of time; it is used *after* an adjective (**a long while**), after a preposition (**for a while**) or after an adverb (**quite a while**).

bare/bear

bare: literally, you can **bare your bottom**, i.e. uncover it, to receive, say, an injection; figuratively, you can also **bare your soul**, in which case you're revealing your innermost thoughts and feelings. When the literal and figurative intersect, though, the result could be this sort of thing: the headline of a newspaper poster is emblazoned with *Film Star Bares All* – the ambiguity, and deception, should be pretty obvious!

bear: has any number of meanings, one being **to put up with** or **tolerate something or someone**, e.g. **He was able to bear his illness with great fortitude**. The past tense of 'bear' is 'bore' (**He bore his illness with great fortitude**), with 'borne' as the past participle (**He has borne his illness ...** etc.) The word 'bear' also, of course, refers to the animal.

begin/start

Use **start** for physical movement (**start to run, start to**

train), **begin** for virtually everything else (**begins with the letter 's'/to begin a field of study**).

between ... and

Use 'and' not 'or' after **between** in this construction: **They had to decide between John or Peter.** (Wrong – change *or* to *and*).

biannual/biennial

biannual: occurring twice a year

biennial: an event taking place every two years

blond/blonde

Use **blond** for men and **blonde** for women; but, when referring to men and women collectively use **blond**; and, **a family of blonds**.

callous/callus

callous: cruel and unfeeling (**callous action**)

callus: hardened skin (**calluses on the heel**)

Sometimes used interchangeably, but stick to the above, although **his calloused heels** is generally accepted.

can/could and may/might

can/could: suggest capability, e.g. **He can do it./He discovered he could cope.**

may/might: suggests being allowed to (**may**), or some form of possibility (**might**), e.g. **You may leave the room./He might succeed, if he puts his mind to it.**

centre/middle

Use **centre** for 'mathematical' references (**the centre of a sphere/the centre of the universe**) or for figurative use (**the centre of attraction**); retain **middle** for the more ordinary or commonplace (**the man in the middle/the middle of the day**).

centre in/centre on

You can **centre on** or **centre in** but not **centre around** (logically, this is, of course, impossible!) In colloquial usage, though, the latter is (unfortunately) gaining ground.

compare to/compare with

compare to: refers to having something in common. (**She has been compared to an angel.**)

compare with: refers to both similarities and differences, with the greater weight being given to the latter. (**The new goalkeeper can't compare with his predecessor, when it comes to ability.**)

complement/compliment

complement: something that completes, or goes satisfactorily with something else, e.g. **Cheese is a perfect complement to a meal**.

compliment: to express praise, approval or admiration, e.g. **Jackson complimented Jennifer on her hairdo**.

comprises/consists of

As **comprises** means 'consists of', it is ungrammatical to have it followed by 'of', e.g. **comprises of / is comprised of**. Thus, 'The team **is comprised of** six players and a manager' is wrong: instead, replace **is comprised of** with **comprises**.

concave/convex

concave: curved inwards like the inside surface of a ball ⌣

convex: curved like the outside surface of a ball ⌒

contagious/infectious

contagious: a disease spread by contact with another person

infectious: a disease caused by bacteria i.e. microscopic organism that exist in air, water, etc.

continual/continuous

> **continual** means 'repeatedly happening', while **continuous** means 'happening uninterruptedly'.

> Thus a 'continual noise' refers to several occurrences of noise *with breaks between them*, while 'continuous noise' refers to noise that goes on for a period of time *without pause or break*.

councillor/counsellor

> councillor: an elected member of a town or city council

> counsellor: an adviser, e.g. **a marriage counsellor**

currently/presently

> Sometimes difficult to decide which is which, so, stick with these meanings: **currently** means *at the present time* (**He's currently overseas.**), while **presently** means *after a short while* or *soon* (**The director will be with you presently**.)

desert/dessert

> desert: barren land, with little water and vegetation; 'to desert' means **leave**, **abandon**, **go away from**, etc.

> dessert: any pudding, tart, ice-cream, etc. eaten to round off a meal

different from/different to

Either is correct, but avoid the American form of **different than**.

disc/disk

A **disc** is any 'flat, thin, round object'; a **disk**, on the other hand, is an 'information storage device for a computer' – it is also flat, thin and round. Note the use of 'disc' in **disc jockey** and **disc brakes**, but of 'disk' in **disk drive** and **diskette**, the latter two because they are associated with computers.

discomfit/discomfort

discomfort: to feel a slight pain or a little uncomfortable, e.g. **Holly still suffers a bit of discomfort in her side after the operation**.

discomfit: to be made upset or uneasy, e.g. **Roger was discomfited by the rejection of his proposal of marriage**.

discreet/discrete

discreet: to be careful in speech or behaviour, e.g. **We must be discreet in our enquiries**.

discrete: distinct and separate, e.g. **a sequence of discrete incidents**

The spelling of these words is often confused; the good news is, however, that you'll probably never find yourself having to use 'discrete'! So, remember, it's a double **ee** when you're being careful in what you say or do!

disinterested/uninterested

These two words once had the same meaning; however, this is no longer the case.

disinterested: neutral, objective, having no interest in something, e.g. **He was a disinterested bystander**, i.e. *impartial, not involved.*

uninterested: not interested, indifferent, e.g. **He was quite uninterested in what was being discussed**, i.e. *not interested in,* or *not concerned about.*

draft/draught

draft: to make a rough, initial version of something, e.g. **a draft plan, a first draft of a book**

draught: current of coolish air in a room or confined space, e.g. **to feel a draught at the back of one's head**

Both words have other meanings, but these are the two most often confused.

dreamed/dreamt

Both spellings are correct.

egoist/egotist

egoist: refers to a selfish person, i.e. one consumed by self-interest.

egotist: is a person who talks too much or too often about himself, i.e. it's always 'I this' and 'I that'!

Examples of usage: **He is an egoist**; and **He is an egotist** – I hope this is helpful!

elicit/illicit

elicit: to try to draw something (e.g. a statement) out of somebody, i.e. **elicit a response**

illicit: illegal, i.e. **illicit diamond buying**

eligible/illegible

eligible: a suitable person, i.e. **an eligible bachelor/to be eligible for higher rank**

illegible: unclear, almost impossible to read, i.e. **an illegible handwriting**

emigrant/immigrant

An **emigrant** is one **who leaves his own country** to settle in another; an **immigrant** is someone **who comes to a foreign country** to live there permanently.

eminent/imminent

eminent: a famous, distinguished person

imminent: likely to happen soon

Two in one: **The eminent scientist's retirement is imminent.**

enquire/inquire

May be used interchangeably, but **inquire** seems to be used more often. For interest's sake only, we can distinguish between 'to enquire about' (i.e. **ask about**) and 'to inquire into' (i.e. **to find out about something**).

Two in one: **He was told to inquire into what the job entailed and, then, once satisfied, to enquire about the salary.**

entomology/etymology

entomology: scientific study of insects

etymology: a study of the origins and history in the meaning of a word

epigram/epigraph/epitaph

epigram: a short, clever and amusing saying or poem

epigraph: a quotation at the beginning of a book and, sometimes, a chapter epitaph: words written on a gravestone

envelop/envelope

envelop: to wrap something up; to cover or surround it completely

envelope: a flat paper container, with a gummed, sealable flap, used for letters, etc.

farther/further

Both mean the same thing, but **further** is the preferred choice.

fewer/less

Use **fewer** for **number** (**fewer enrolments, fewer people than before**), and **less** for **quantity** or **amount** (**add less flour, drink less wine**), as a general rule. However, if a *singular noun* follows, use **less** (**less choice**), but if a *plural noun* follows, use **fewer** (**fewer choices**).

first/firstly

If items in a list are numbered, use either **first, ... second, ... third, ...** etc. or **firstly, ... secondly, ... thirdly, ...** etc. as either is acceptable. Avoid, though, as some insist on doing, **first, ... secondly, ... thirdly, ...** etc.

flaunt/flout

flaunt: to show off, e.g. your wealth, etc.

flout: openly to disobey, e.g. an order, a rule, etc.

Two in one: **If you've got it, flaunt it, but take care not to flout the code of common decency**.

forbear/forebear

Forbear, in the sense of 'to stop oneself from doing or saying something while showing annoyance or complaint' is now a bit old-fashioned. It can, though, be used interchangeably with **forebear**, referring to one's ancestors (**our forebears/forbears were originally from ...**); however, **forebear** is the preferred word.

Two in one: **You must forbear from criticising your forebears**.

gaol/jail

Either may be used for a place of imprisonment.

genetic/generic

genetic: having to do with the way in which characteristics are passed on from parents, or parent stock, to their offspring, e.g. **genetic defect**

generic:

- refers to a class or group; not specific, e.g. **The generic term for cabbages, peas, beans, and so on, is vegetables.**

- refers to medical drugs no longer protected by a trade mark, e.g. **generic medicines.**

gourmand/gourmet

A **gourmand** is a glutton, i.e. a person who eats too much; a **gourmet** is someone who knows a lot about, and enjoys, good food and wine.

gray/grey

Either may be used, but **grey** is the more popular.

gypsy/gipsy

Both are correct.

hangar/hanger

A **hangar** is the building in which aeroplanes are housed; a **hanger** is the frame on which clothes are hung up.

hanged/hung

The murderer was hanged (never **hung**), *BUT*, **The curtains were hung./The clothes were hung up to dry.**

historic/historical

historic: memorable, famous or important in history, e.g. **Yesterday will be remembered as a historic day, as it was the first time in years that South Africa beat Australia in a cricket test**.

historical: of or concerning history, e.g. **She writes historical novels**.

homophone/homonym

homophone: a word pronounced the same as some other word but with a different spelling or meaning, e.g. **cord/chord**.

homonym: a word with the same spelling and pronunciation as another but with a different meaning, e.g. **rest** (**a well-earned rest**) and **rest** (**the rest of the food**).

hopefully

Many purists object to the use of 'hopefully' (as a sentence adverb) to mean 'it is to be hoped that', e.g. **Hopefully, we'll be able to attend the meeting**. This usage is so common these days that it's almost achieved acceptable status. However, use it sparingly, thus, hopefully, reducing the ire of those who object to its use!

imply/infer

imply: to hint at something; to suggest something, not state it directly, e.g. **Are you implying that he stole the money?**

infer: to conclude; to reach a conclusion based on facts or observation, e.g. **To infer, from what you've just said, that he stole the money, is unjust and unfair**.

Do not use **infer** in the sense of **to imply** or **to suggest**; instead, use one or other of the latter words.

ingenious/ingenuous

ingenious: showing cleverness and originally, e.g. **an ingenious plan**

ingenuous: being open and honest, in an innocent, almost childlike, way, e.g. **an ingenuous attitude to life**

judgement/judgment

Both are correct, but I prefer **judgement**.

lie/lay

lie:

- **to lie down**, i.e. 'to have a rest'. For this meaning, the correct past tenses are: **lying down**, **lay down** and **has lain down**.

- **to lie**, i.e. 'not to tell the truth'. The past
  tenses are **is lying**, **has lied**, **will have lied**.

lay: **to lay off workers**, i.e. 'to get rid of workers'. Here, the past tenses are: **have been laying** off workers, **have laid** off workers, **will have laid off** workers.

It is, therefore, wrong to say **Mathilda has been laying** (i.e. lying) **on the couch all afternoon** or **Locksley has laid** (i.e. lain) **on the couch all afternoon**. Remember, too, that a chicken has **laid**, not **lain**, an egg!

lighted/lit

Use either, no matter what you hear to the contrary: **He lighted/lit Jemima's cigarette; a well-lighted/ well-lit place**.

lightening/lightning

The sky is lightening (getting lighter), *BUT*, **There's a lot of lightning and thunder**.

liqueur/liquor

liqueur: a strong alcoholic drink, usually sweetened

liquor: an alcoholic drink, especially spirits such as whisky, brandy, gin

meantime/mean time

Write as one word (**in the meantime**) in almost all cases. As two words, **mean time** has a few specialised applications only (**Greenwich Mean Time**).

orientated/oriented

Both are correct. **The business is strongly oriented/ orientated towards customer satisfaction**.

palate/pallet/palette

palate: roof of the mouth

pallet: a wooden platform for carrying goods, usually lifted or lowered by a fork-lift truck

palette: a board on which an artist mixes his paints

passed/past

passed: is used as a verb, e.g. **He passed me by.**

past: is used adjectivally, e.g. **in past times** (it 'describes' or qualifies the noun 'times'); as a preposition, e.g. **The next bus leaves at ten past six**; or, as an adverb, e.g. **He dashed past me** (it modifies the verb 'dashed').

pedal/peddle

pedal: foot-operated levers that power, for instance, a

bicycle, e.g. **He pedalled furiously down the hill**.

peddle: to try to sell things by going from (mainly) house to house, e.g. **He was peddling sewing kits**. A person involved in this sort of thing is a **pedlar** – or **peddler**!

per cent/percent

Use **per cent** as both an adverb (**a ten per cent decrease in sales**) and a noun (**a return of half a per cent**). It may also be written as one word (**percent**) when used as a noun, but this is optional; therefore, stick with **per cent**. **Percentage** is always written as one word.

racist/racialist

Both are correct, as are **racism** and **racialism**. The shorter form, however, has become more acceptable.

rack/wrack

A **rack** can be **a shelf**, **an instrument of torture**, or **something that can cause pain or doubt**, etc. The best-known figurative usage is in **to rack one's brains**, i.e. to think hard in order to bring something back to mind.

Wrack hardly features these days except, as dictionaries helpfully point out, when referring to a kind of seaweed. So, you're quite safe in retaining **rack** for all seasons, even in an expression such as **rack and ruin**, where **wrack** used to be the preferred word.

Scot/Scotch

A **Scot** is a native or inhabitant of Scotland. **Scotch** is another name for **whisky**. Thus, you may order a **Scotch and water** from a **Scotsman**, but never from a **Scotchman**, because there is no such being! Notice, by the way, that **whisky**, without an **e**, is from **Scotland**, but with an **e** (i.e. **whiskey**) is either from **Ireland** or **North America**. You might also come across **Scotch broth**, or a **Scotch egg**, or even **Scotch mist**; then again, it doesn't matter whether you get bitten by a **Scotch terrier** or a **Scots terrier**, as either is correct – and the bite equally painful!

shall/will

The following table explains the difference in usage between these words when preceded by a pronoun; the first column refers to a statement of fact, an assertion, etc. usually about some future event, while the second is used to convey a promise, a threat, an expression of determination, etc.

Fact	Determination
I shall	I will
he will	he shall

we shall	we will
you will	you shall
they will	they shall

Thus, **I shall see you tomorrow** states a *fact*, whereas **I will see you tomorrow** conveys your *determination* to do so.

should/would

Very broadly, **shall = should, will = would: I should be able to cope** (an assertion); **We would like to object in the strongest terms** (determination). (For further specific information, consult a dictionary.)

stalactite/stalagmite

stalactite: a tapering mass of calcium carbonate, in the shape of an icicle, that **hangs** from the roof of a cave (remember – it clings 'tite-ly' to the roof!)

stalagmite: a tapering mass of calcium carbonate, like an icicle, that **rises** from the floor of a cave (remember – it 'mite' reach the roof!)

storey/story

A **storey** refers to the 'floor' of a building (**He lives on the second storey** (floor) **of the building**). Under the influence of US usage, **storey** is nowadays being used interchangeably with **story**. I don't like this – rather stick with **storey**.

till/until

Either is acceptable; however, avoid a phrase like **up until**, as **up** is superfluous: **He worked until the age of eighty**, not **up until**.

unique

This means 'without equal', 'unparalleled'. As such, it is illogical to qualify it with words like *absolutely*, *more*, *very*, *most*, etc., as something is either unique or it's not. However, it has almost become common practice to qualify 'unique' with words such as those above. Perhaps, accept this usage in ordinary speech, but preferably not in formal writing.

venal/venial/venous/vernal

venal: corrupt, open to bribery (**a venal act**)

venial: forgivable, excusable (**a venial sin**)

venous: to do with the veins (**venous blood**)

vernal: refers to the season of spring (**vernal winds**)

waive/wave

waive: to forego, to give up a claim to (**to waive one's rights**)

wave: **a wave in the sea/to wave goodbye**

wander/wonder

wander: to walk about, with no particular place in mind (**He likes to wander in the countryside.**)

wonder: to be amazed or surprised by something (**to be filled with wonder**); to be uncertain about something (**I wonder what's going to happen to us?**)

Hyphens

The author of the style-book of the Oxford University Press of New York (quoted in Perrin's Writer's Guide*) strikes the same note when he says 'If you take hyphens seriously you will surely go mad.'*

The Complete Plain Words – SIR ERNEST GOWERS

Of course, he's absolutely right! And especially now that the tendency is to drop the hyphen between compound words and spell them either as one or two words. The word **dining room** is often instanced as an example of this. It can be written as two words (as in the previous sentence), or as a hyphenated word (**dining-room**) or as one word (**diningroom**). Therefore, when in doubt, consult a dictionary, and, then, for the sake of consistency, stick to the usage in that particular one for all compounds.

(i) One of the functions of the hyphen is to steer clear of ambiguity. A famous example of this is the word **co-op**: it requires the hyphen when referring to a cooperative organisation, otherwise it would be read as **coop** i.e. a cage where poultry is kept – certainly not the intended meaning. Then there's the word **re-lay**, as in to **re-lay a carpet** (i.e. to lay it again, perhaps in a slightly different way): here the hyphen is essential, for, as one word (i.e. **relay**), it means, say, to **transmit,** or relay, **a message**. Then there's the well-known phrase **a man eating fish**. As it stands, it refers to a man enjoying a meal of fish; but if a hyphen is inserted between **man** and **eating** (**man-eating fish**), the meaning changes dramatically, for the reference is now to a fish that hunts and eats people!

(ii) With technical and similar terms, the hyphen is also, understandably, sometimes used to guard against even a whiff of ambivalence, as in, for instance, the word **light-year**, which is the means of measuring the distance between stars and galaxies. Without the hyphen, the implication could well be that the year was either not heavy or not dark! (But, change is once again in the air, with the result that the hyphen, in this case, no longer seems obligatory.)

(iii) The hyphen is used in compounds such as the following:
- **mother-in-law**, **mother-of-pearl**, **pay-as-you-earn**, but not in **next of kin**, **arm in arm**, **coat of arms** (for some obscure reason or other).
- for compound adjectives, i.e. when describing a noun, e.g. **a well-known man**; however, if it follows a verb and performs another function, it is not hyphenated, e.g. **He is particularly well known for his charitable deeds**.
- when two nouns are grouped as a unit, e.g. **player-manager**, **actor-director**; also

when used adjectivally, in instances such as
Anglo-American War.

- for most prefixes beginning with **self** (**self-proclaimed**), **all** (**all-round**), **quasi** (**quasi-scientific**), **pro** (**pro-South African**), and so on.
- for a suffix such as **elect** (**president-elect**).
- when a prefix ends with the same letter as the initial letter to which it is joined, e.g. **semi-independent**, **pre-empt**, **re-educate**; in some cases, though, the tendency is to drop the hyphen, as in **cooperate** (or **co-operate**), **coordinate** (or **co-ordinate**).
- for the prefix **anti**, e.g. **anti-inflammatory**, **anti-American**, *BUT* **anti-Semitic** or **antisemitic**.
- when an upper case letter is joined to a noun, e.g. **A-bomb**, **X-ray**.
- when a suffix is joined to a proper noun, e.g. **Einstein-like moustache**.
- for **bull's-eye** (the centre spot on a board for darts, or a kind of hard sweet) and **cat's-eye** (a kind of semi-precious stone) – although, according to the *SA Concise Oxford*, only **bullseye** is acceptable, while **catseye** is the trademark name for a light-reflecting device set into a road. On the other hand, there's

crow's-nest (apostrophe and hyphen),
BUT **rat's tails** (apostrophe only – meaning long, greasy strands of hair). Confusing? Of course, *BUT* that's English for you!

- for numbers from **twenty-one** to **ninety-nine**.

(iv) A hyphen is used for simple fractions when spelt out: **three-quarters**, **nine-tenths**, **one-third**.

(v) **a newly minted coin, a truly great man**

Please note that there is NO hyphen after the **ly** word in this, very common, construction, i.e. where an adverb ending in **ly** (**newly**, **truly**), modifies an adjective (**minted**, **great**), which in turn qualifies a noun (**coin**, **man**).

(vi) Do not leave a hyphen hanging in 'mid-air' as in:
You can either book me into a first- or second-class compartment.
Instead, write ... **into a first-class or second-class compartment.**

Italics and Quotation Marks

'My dear Mr Bennet,' replied his wife,
'how can you be so tiresome!
You must know that I am thinking of his
marrying one of them.'

Pride and Prejudice – JANE AUSTEN

Italics

To Aldus Manutius (1449-1515), an Italian printer based in Venice from 1490, belongs the distinction of having invented italic type. For those interested in such things, any good dictionary will tell you that it derives from Greek **Italikos**, from Latin **Italia** Italy, and refers, as we know, to a typeface that slopes to the right.

Italics are used for:
- the titles of books (*The Great Gatsby*), plays (*Romeo and Juliet*), films (*Downfall*), operas (*The Magic Flute*), works of art (the *Mona Lisa*), newspapers (*The Star*), magazines (*Femina*), very long poems (*Paradise Lost*).
- foreign words (*bambino*) and phrases (*bon soir*), except when they have become 'naturalised', e.g. 'carpe diem', 'bon vivant'. The latter is also true of Afrikaans words that have become a part of South African English; therefore, words such as 'veld', 'koppie', 'trek', 'stoep', etc., need not be italicised.
- emphasis: 'Are you *still* talking?'
- the names of ships (*Queen Mary II*),

boats (**Marilyn**), excluding HMS, e.g.
HMS *Endeavour*.

- focusing attention on a letter (the letter *t*)
  or a word (the word ***centre***).
- scientific names from the Latin for birds
  (***Charadrius tricollaris*** – Threebanded
  Plover), plants (***Nepeta mussinii*** –
  Catmint).

Quotation Marks

(i) Quotation marks and roman (i.e. ordinary) type are used for:
- names of articles when quoted from newspapers or magazines (in the article **'Ten Killed in Flash Flood'** ...)
- names of chapters of books (Chapter 1 of *Cranford* by Mrs Gaskell is entitled **'Our Society'**.)
- names of essays (One of the essays in Edmund Wilson's book *Classics and Commercials* is **'Ambushing a Best-Seller'**.)
- names of poems (T S Eliot's **'The Waste Land'**.)

(Note that the books of the Bible are neither italicised nor enclosed in quotation marks, thus, **Genesis**, **Exodus**, **Hebrews**.*)*

(ii) Direct speech
This refers to the actual words spoken by someone, such as a character in a novel or short story. The words are enclosed in quotation marks, sometimes called inverted commas. Either single or double quotes may be used, although the tendency these

days is towards the former. The quotation marks may either be roman ('...') or inverted commas ('...').

Punctuation marks must be placed within the inverted comma:

'It's time to leave,' said Caroline.

Caroline said, 'It's time to leave.'

In the first sentence, the speech verb ('said') is written with a small letter, as it follows a comma. In the second sentence, the name of the speaker ('Caroline') and the speech verb take a following comma to indicate that something is still to come, namely, a sentence of direct speech, which, as it is a sentence, takes an initial capital. Even if the direct speech consists of one word only, the first letter is always upper case:

Jemima responded with an emphatic, 'No!'

Exclamation and question marks, terminating direct speech, are also inserted within the inverted comma:

'Hurry up!' exclaimed Caroline.

Caroline asked, 'Is it time to leave?'

The following two sentences are among the most common to be found in novels, short stories, etc. Carefully note the difference in punctuation between them:

'Let us,' said Caroline, 'leave early.'

'Let us leave now,' said Caroline. 'It's getting late.'

In the first example, the name of the speaker ('Caroline')

and the speech verb ('said') divide a *single sentence* into two parts: in such instances, a comma follows the name of the speaker – or speech verb, as the case might be – and the sentence continues with a small letter (leave). In the second example, the speech verb and name of speaker separate *two sentences*, thus a full stop follows the name of the speaker and the next sentence begins with a capital (It's).

If a speaker speaks a number of consecutive *sentences* (i.e. without any form of interruption between them), the inverted comma is closed only after the last sentence, i.e. there are no inverted commas between sentences:

> **'Let us leave now. It's getting late. And you know we've got to be at the airport by six,'
> said Caroline.**

On the other hand, if a speaker speaks a number of consecutive *paragraphs*, an inverted comma opens each paragraph, but is only closed after the final paragraph: in other words, there is no inverted comma at the end of each paragraph, except, as stated, after the final one:

> **'Come on. Get a move on now. We *must* get going. You know we've got to be at the airport by six at the latest.**
>
> **'No! Definitely not. Not even one more drink. Not even a sip. There's just no time.**
>
> **'You know, you're the world's worst. If it**

were up to you, we'd be late for everything.
Yes, everything. Remember the last time we
had to catch a plane? We made it by the skin
of our teeth. And it's not going to happen this
time again. That's for absolute sure.'

Double inverted commas are used for a quote within a
quote (i.e. where single inverted commas are used for the
direct speech):

'He said "I'm definitely not going" when I
spoke to him yesterday,' Caroline muttered.

If the quote within a quote comes at the end of the
sentence, the final comma is inserted between the
concluding inverted commas:

'He said "I'm definitely not going",' Caroline
muttered.

Note the position of the final full stop in each of the
following:

- I think Michele Ciaramella was
  absolutely right in suggesting that 'The
  tradition inaugurated by Bacon was
  continued throughout the 17th Century
  by philosophers who achieved world-
  wide and lasting fame.'
- Michele Ciaramella said that it was John
  Locke who had originated the theory

of the social contract 'as the basis of government'.

If a statement ends with a longish, or full sentence quote, as in the first example, the full stop is inserted *within* the final inverted comma. If, though, it ends with a shortish, or phrasal quote, the full stop is placed *outside* the concluding inverted comma. Purely for the sake of 'neatness', some insist on *always* having the full stop within the inverted comma, no matter what sort of sentence structure it is. I do not agree, but the choice is yours.

Numbers, Figures
and the Date

'That's not a regular rule: you invented it just now.'

'It's the oldest rule in the book,' said the King.

'Then it ought to be Number One,' said Alice.

Alice in Wonderland – LEWIS CARROLL

I never made exceptions. An exception disproves the rule.

Dr Watson in *The Sign of the Four* – SIR ARTHUR CONAN DOYLE

Are there such things as 'regular rules'? Most definitely. And are there rules that are the oldest 'in the book'? Of course. And are there any 'Number One' rules? Any number, I should think, as it's well nigh impossible to rank rules in order of importance, for most cannot but be, in one way or another, a Number One rule. However, as we know, there are sometimes exceptions to rules. And, despite Dr Watson's intransigence in the matter, an exception, far from disproving the rule, might actually do the opposite, i.e. by creating a new one. In the light of all of this, it is not surprising, then, that this section should begin with the words 'As a general rule – there are exceptions – '

(i) As a general rule – there are exceptions – spell out numbers up to ninety-nine, especially if used adjectivally, but use figures for 100 and higher:

At least twenty-nine people were killed in the accident.

There were at least 150 people at the meeting.

(Remember that all compound numbers between twenty-one and ninety-nine are hyphenated.)

(ii) Spell out words above 100 if they make up no more than two words:

He was elected by a slim majority of about two hundred votes.

BUT **The final count gave him the victory by no more than 179 votes.**

(iii) A number should not begin or end a sentence; instead use words, or re-arrange the sentence:
Two hundred and three (not 203) **strikers were fined.**
Amazingly, he has recently turned one hundred.

(iv) Money and years, given in figures, may end but rather not begin a sentence:
He was owed R29.
He died in 1926.

(v) If usage is indefinite, spell out all numbers:
more than one hundred and fifty per cent, hundreds of ideas, thousands of years.

(vi) Even if numbers are below ninety-nine, use figures in order to avoid a succession of hyphens:
21-year-old ten-ton truck
NOT **twenty-one-year-old ten-ton truck.**

(vii) Use words for idiomatic, etc. language:
to be given six of the best, ten to one, one in a million, the First Eleven, two dozen eggs, one-ton truck.

(viii) A distinction is sometimes drawn between

formal and informal usage, especially in respect of time, money, weight, percentages, and so on. This table illustrates the point; however, whether you go along with it, or not, is entirely up to you:

Informal	Formal
7 o'clock or 7 p.m.	seven o'clock
R7-50	seven rands and fifty cents
69 per cent (or %)	sixty-nine per cent
250 g	two hundred and fifty grams
BUT 21°C rather than	twenty-one degrees Celsius

(ix) For addresses, where the name of the street is a number, write in words if under nine, but in figures if higher than that:

7 Seventh Street *BUT* 11 21st Street

(x) Ages should be given in figures:

6 months old, 7 years old, aged 63

(xi) Figures are used for sport scores:

Cats defeat Sharks 26 – 10

and for horse racing odds:

a 4-1 odds-on favourite

and for these:

Act 1 Sc. 2, Chapter 24, page 123, Radio 702, 4 on the Richter scale, Room 6

and for mathematical usage:

add 6 and 6, multiply by 6, subtract 7 from 11

(xii) For pages, dates, etc. use a minimum number of figures:

45-7, 1526-8, 1526-84

However, figures between 10 and 19 must be kept intact:

11-15, 1517-19

Give dates in full when one century switches to another:

1636-1719

(xiii) In **formal usage**, dates should always be given in full, i.e. **16 September 1958**. No ordinal abbreviation (**th, rd, st**) should follow the day of the month. The definite article (i.e. **the**) should not precede the year, thus:

I met him at 6 p.m. on 21 May 2001.

If only the day of the month is given, it must be spelt out in full and be preceded by the definite article:

I met him on the twelfth.

In **informal usage**, these months may be abbreviated:

Jan., Feb., Aug., Sept., Oct., Nov., Dec., but not **March, April, May, June, July:**

6 Jan. 2006 or **6 Jan. '06** or **Jan. 6, '06**

The date may also consist of figures only:

6-6-2006 or **06-06-2006** or **2006-06-06**

(These should only be used for the date on cheques and such-like.)

PS There are those who prefer nine (not ninety-nine) as the cut-off point for words, with figures for 10 (not 100) and higher, thus: **There were 15 people in attendance, eight women and seven men**. If this is more to your liking, go for it! All you've got to do is to make the necessary adjustments – where applicable – to the above 'rules'.

Punctuation

I hate quotations

Journals, 13 April 1834 – RALPH WALDO EMERSON

Comma

As we know, the main use of the comma is to point out a short break between parts of a sentence or to separate items in a list. When it comes to specifics, though, there is much more to be said about it, much of it both tedious and – yes – ultimately unnecessary. Instead, then, only some of its more generally accepted functions will be tackled in what follows.

(i) It separates a series of adjectives that qualify a noun:

The tall, noisy, well-built man

(Do not use a comma after the last adjective.)

Some writers these days omit the commas altogether:

The tall noisy well-built man

(I prefer the commas.)

(ii) It separates a list of nouns:

Toyotas, Mercedes, BMWs and Fiats were showcased.

(A comma before 'and' is optional, but the tendency is to omit it. The word **showcased** can also be written as one word.)

(iii) Insert a comma – or commas – for **of course**, **in fact**, **I think**, **however**, **too**, etc. when used parenthetically:

It was, of course, unlikely.

He, too, was there.

However, it was unnecessary.

It's not, I think, like that.

(Once again, some writers leave out the commas; if you decide to do so, though, do so consistently. However, I much prefer the commas.)

(iv) Also use commas for **yes, no, please**:

Yes, I would like that.

No, I will not go.

Two sugars, please.

BUT **Please stop doing that.**

(v) Use a comma – or commas – to separate the name of the person addressed from the rest of the sentence:

Andrew, please come here.

Please, Andrew, come here.

BUT **Jack strolled into the room.**

The same applies to a name replaced by an attribute:

Silly, there's no need to cry.

BUT **He's really a silly boy.**

(vi) Use commas between titles or degrees after a person's name:

T Q S Reilly, BA, MA, MEd

(vii) Use a comma – or commas – for participial

phrases (*see page 43*):

**Standing on the crest of the mountain, he
looked down into the valley.**

Petersen, screaming loudly, rushed at them.

**Frightened by the strength of the current,
Jocelyn decided not to venture any deeper.**

**Having been conned once, she was now wary of
entering into any new contracts.**

*(Some writers omit the comma/commas. That's fine, but
I prefer to retain them.)*

(viii) Use commas for noun phrases or clauses in
apposition:

Ruth, the doctor's daughter, never complains.

**The idea, that we do not accept the invitation,
was unanimously agreed on.**

(ix) Omit commas for defining – i.e. restrictive
– adjectival clauses:

**The girls who were good singers were first to
leave.** (i.e. *only* the girls who were good singers
were the first to leave – the clause *defines* which of
the girls were the first to leave.)

BUT, use commas for non-defining – i.e. non-restrictive
– adjectival clauses:

**The girls, who were good singers, were the first
to leave.** (i.e. *all* of the girls were good singers, and

all were the first to leave – the clause is *not restricted* to only some of the girls.)

(x) A comma is used to mark off adverbial clauses, i.e. clauses that modify a verb (these usually begin with **when, while, after, as soon as, where, for, since, as, because, so that, if, unless, provided that, though, although, even though, so, so ... that, as much as, as far as, as if**):
When he arrived, he was ushered inside.
Provided that you leave early, you should have no problem with the traffic.
He spoke confidently, as if he had all the answers.
(Once again, let it be said, some writers omit the comma. Please don't!)

(xi) Then there's the vexed question of the comma before 'and' or 'but' (and the other co-ordinate conjunctions), when these introduce (longish) phrases and clauses. Some writers use it, some don't:
He had committed himself to writing the article, and then regretted doing so. (*Author, Author* – David Lodge)
She took a deep breath and looked him in the eye. (*Winter in Madrid* – C J Sansom)

The rule is simple: either you use it, or you don't, but be consistent; if not, you could end up with something like this:

> **He and his mother had not been close before his father died and even this had not changed their relationship for the better. In fact, he saw much more of his grandmother, and this irked his mother no end.**

The structure of both sentences is reasonably similar, so there's no earthly reason why a comma should feature in the one and not in the other.

However, note the following:

- **Justin and Eve arrived early**. (No commas)
- **The work is hard but the hours aren't long**. (No comma before 'but' is necessary, unless you're going to use it consistently in all sentences of a similar kind.)
- **John, and perhaps Eve, will be there**. (Commas may be used for an *aside*, as in this instance.)
- **The sailors were not gentlemen, and the gentlemen were not sailors**. (A comma, in this well-known sentence, is almost obligatory; therefore, use it when one part of the sentence, as in this example, *is balanced by the other*.)

(To say more would be to go round in circles, which is likely to confuse rather than clarify. Anyhow, I think there's enough for now.)

(xii) Use commas to separate a number of related
words, phrases or clauses coming after one
another:
**In the Kruger Park, we saw lions, elephants,
giraffes and crocodiles.** (Words)
**Herbert will be working with a few NGOs, with
quite a number of corporates, with at least one
government department and with a legal firm.**
(Phrases)
**In a lifetime of adventure, she has swum with
dolphins, she has abseiled down mountains, she
has climbed Kilimanjaro and has even driven
from Cape to Cairo.** (Clauses)

(xiii) Use a comma to separate infinitive or
prepositional phrases from the main clause of
the sentence:
**To accomplish anything in life, you have to be
absolutely dedicated.** (Infinitive phrase)
**In order to succeed, you must be properly
motivated.** (Prepositional phrase)

Colon

Its main function is to show that something is to follow, e.g. an explanation, an expansion, a list of things, etc.:

We bought the following: two pencils; two boxes of paper clips; a dozen rulers; and three pens.
There were a number of alternatives: buy, sell, or wait.

(Note that the colon should not follow a verb:

Our order is: one ham and cheese sandwich ...)

The first word after the colon, as in the two examples above, are lower-cased. This is the rule, unless a full sentence follows:

He made it very clear: We will never give up.

A colon is used after the words 'follows' or 'following'. The book is sprinkled with many such examples; in fact, you've only to look at this very section for confirmation of this.

Semicolon

(i) It separates items in a list, especially if coming after a colon (refer to the first example under Colon above).

(ii) It separates a series of co-ordinate clauses, i.e. when they are not linked by co-ordinate conjunctions (*and*, *but*, *or*, *nor*):
The room was packed; the speaker was compelling; the audience was enthralled.

(Here the semicolons take the place of 'and'.)

(iii) It separates a number of subordinate clauses of the same kind:
He was the sort of person who never stopped talking; who rubbed everyone up the wrong way; and who always exuded an air of the utmost pessimism.

(The subordinate clauses are adjectival.)

(iv) When a sentence consists of two statements and the second is merely an extension of the first, the two are separated by a semicolon:
I spoke to him last night; he was more optimistic than ever before.

(v) When the second of two main clauses in
a sentence is introduced by words such
'however', 'of course', 'in fact', 'basically', etc.,
a semicolon is inserted after the first clause:
He promised never to do that again; however,
I still do not fully trust him.
We trusted him completely; of course, we
were naive to do so, given his past history.
(Note that in structures such as these a comma always
follows 'however', 'of course', etc.)

Full stop

It is used, as we all know, at the end of sentences that are neither exclamations nor questions. It is also used for certain abbreviations, as already fully discussed.

Exclamation mark

(i) It indicates an exclamation and is usually placed at the end of a sentence:
Well, I never!

(ii) It is used to convey strong emotion:
Don't you ever do that again!

(iii) It can also be used to emphasise something:
You must stop doing that, immediately!

(iv) In certain instances, an exclamation mark can over-ride a question mark, i.e. the sentence is undoubtedly a question, but the exclamatory element is stronger:
Wasn't that a great passage of play!

(v) It follows an interjection:
Phew! I really thought we weren't going to make it.

(vi) Writers can use the exclamation mark to share with the reader something they found amusing, startling or surprising:
I can't believe that he's broken his leg again!
(I've used this particular device quite liberally in the book – although frowned on by some, I happen to like using it!)

Question mark

(i) It terminates a direct question:
How old are you?

(ii) Each sentence in a series takes a question mark:
Are we going to throw in the towel? Are we just going to give up without a fight? Are we really that weak? Of course, not!

(iii) For a question not posed directly, use a question mark, not a full stop:
I'm not sure, but I wonder whether you're the right person to ask?

Dash

The en-rule – this refers to the *short* dash and is used as follows:

- in pairs as brackets, e.g. **The predominant trees – jacaranda, oak, pine – were all destined to be cut down**.
- to introduce additional information to what has gone before, e.g. **It was a truly great idea – one that could bring in much-needed capital**.
- for some form of movement from one thing to another: **1914–1918 War, Johannesburg–Bloemfontein–Cape Town route**, etc.

The em-rule – this refers to the *long* dash. It is used to indicate that a speaker has been interrupted or has not completed her sentence; this means that it is sometimes used in place of an **ellipsis (...)**, e.g. **You tell me. Why didn't he pitch up? What sort of game is ——**

Another of its functions is to replace the omitted part of a word, e.g. **I've never heard such d—— nonsense**.

Spelling

'Do you spell it with a "V" or a "W"?' inquired the judge.
'That depends upon the taste and fancy of the speller, my Lord,'
replied Sam.

The Pickwick Papers – CHARLES DICKENS

If only it were as easy as this, which, of course, it isn't. George Bernard Shaw, the playwright, detested the irregularity of English spelling, and for this reason left a sum of money in his will to be awarded to the person who could produce 'a fit British alphabet containing at least forty-two letters, and thereby capable of noting with sufficient accuracy for recognition all the sounds of spoken English without having to use more than one letter for each sound, which is impossible with the ancient 26-letter Phoenician alphabet at present in use.' (Quoted by Hesketh Pearson in *Bernard Shaw*.) Shaw believed that, if adopted, the new alphabet would, in some way or other, save the country a lot of time and money.

A competition was duly held, and a certain Kingsley Read was declared the winner. The alphabet he produced appears to be – at least, to the thinking person! – nothing less than arbitrary scratch marks on a sheet of notepaper, some the height of upper case, and others of lower case, letters. Needless to say, nothing came of this.

Furthermore, Shaw famously ridiculed English spelling by declaring that, if words were spelt as they were pronounced, the correct way of rendering 'fish' should be 'ghoti' – the 'f' sound deriving from the 'gh' in cou**gh**, the 'i' as in w**o**men, and the 'sh' as in, say, dicta**ti**on!

Now, why is English spelling generally feared? The usual answer, as Shaw has pointed out, is that – by and large – it is not a phonetic language, i.e. words are not spelt according to the way they're pronounced. This is undoubtedly true, for instance, of certain unusual proper and place names, where the pronunciation bears no relation whatever to its spelling. Take, for example, the female name 'Niamb': unless you – or I – had been told beforehand, would we have been able to arrive at its correct pronunciation of **Neeve**? I doubt it. Or what about 'Siobhan', pronounced as **Shi** (as in 'ship') – **vaughn** (that's as close as I can get!) These are first names, but there are a few surnames equally as bad: 'Cholmondeley' is, astonishingly, pronounced as **Chumley**; then there's 'Featherstonehaugh' which can be pronounced in various ways, but generally – and most unlikely – as **Fanshaw**!

These are, of course, extreme cases. Yet, even as simple and well known a place name as 'Worcester' falls four-square into the same category as the ones above, for, once again, its pronunciation, **Wus-ter**, has nothing in common with its spelling. And this is only the tip of the iceberg!

A further problem bedevilling English spelling is where similar pronunciations have different spellings, and where similar spellings have different pronunciations. Here we only have to look at a word such as 'bough' (branch of a tree), which is pronounced the same as 'bow' (to take a bow on stage), which, in turn, is spelt the same as 'bow' (as in bow and arrow) – yet pronounced differently. Or compare 'bough' to 'tough' and 'lough': despite having

–**ough** in common, each sound is unlike the other. This is enough to drive anyone to drink!

One of the reasons for much of this confusion can be laid at the door of the various influences the English language has undergone over past centuries. This has resulted, among other things, in the absorption of a variety of words into English from different cultures, with the original spelling often being either adapted, or left (virtually) unchanged. Therefore, the sound of such words is inevitably at variance with their spelling.

Some of these 'borrowings' entered English from languages such as Spanish, French, Greek, Portuguese and Italian. The word 'bizarre' i.e. **bi'za:ʳ**, a French word from the Spanish **bizarro**, meaning 'gallant' or 'brave', is one such example. It certainly doesn't look or sound like an English word, and, furthermore, now means 'odd' or 'strange'. Compare this to 'bazaar' i.e. **ba'za:** or **ba'zar**, from the Persian, meaning a market. Here we have the same old problem of the often encountered divide between pronunciation and spelling: -**zarre** and –**zaar** are pronounced in more or less the same way, but are spelt differently, in this case, for purely historical reasons.

But, hold on. Are things really as bad as they seem? Is English spelling really as chaotic as all the foregoing would lead us to believe? Fortunately, not so, for there are a sufficiency of useful rules to assist in overcoming many of the problems often associated with English spelling.

Yes, there are exceptions to the rules, but nowhere near enough to render them invalid.

Here, now, are some of the more important ones:

Plurals

(i) Most plurals are formed by adding an **s** to the singular:

aeroplane – aeroplanes

(ii) If a noun ends in a 'hissing' consonant sound, i.e. **sh**, **ch**, **x**, **s**, add an **es** for the plural:

leech – leeches
lash – lashes
gas – gases
fax – faxes

(iii) For most nouns ending in **fe** drop the **fe** and replace with **ves**:

life – lives

(iv) Most nouns ending in **f** take only an **s** for the plural (usually with words of shorter sound):

chief – chiefs (short sound)
BUT **thief – thieves** (longer sound)
roof – roofs (short sound)
BUT **hoof – hoofs** or **hooves**! (oh, dear!)

(v) Words ending in **y** and preceded by a vowel – add an **s**:

storey – storeys

(vi) Words ending in **y** and preceded by a consonant – drop the **y** and replace with **ies**:
story – stories

(vii) There are some irregular plurals:
woman – women

(viii) Some singular nouns remain unchanged in the plural:
salmon – salmon

(ix) In compounds of three words, add an **s** to the 'main' word:
mother-in-law – mothers-in-law
grant-in-aid – grants-in-aid

(x) In certain compounds, regarded as one word, there is generally a choice:
attorneys general or **attorney generals** (no hyphen)
poets laureate or **poet laureates**
BUT **sergeant majors** (with, or without, a hyphen)

(xi) Nouns ending in **o** and preceded by a vowel, add **s**:
cameo – cameos

(xii) Nouns ending in **o** and preceded by a consonant, add **s**:
ego – egos

piano – **pianos**

BUT **es** to words such as: **heroes, potatoes, tomatoes, echoes**

AND **cargos** or **cargoes,** one **buffalo** and a herd of thirty **buffalo** or **buffaloes!**

(xiii) For the plurals of proper names add either an **es** (to names ending in **s**) or **s** (to names ending in other letters of the alphabet):
I paid the **Dickenses** a visit.
I dropped in on the **Smiths**.

(xiv) For the plurals of words ending in **ful** add an **s** to **ful** i.e. not to the 'container' which precedes it:
cupful – cupfuls
teaspoonful – teaspoonfuls
wheelbarrowful – wheelbarrowfuls

(xv) For words from the Latin ending in **us**, add either **es** or drop the **us** and add **i** for the plural:
syllabus – syllabuses or **syllabi**
hippopotamus – hippopotamuses or **hippopotami**
(Despite these allowable alternatives, I much prefer the **es** *ending.)*

(xvi) For words from the Latin ending in **a**, add

either an **s** or an **e** for the plural, depending
on meaning:
antenna – **antennas** (aerials) or **antennae** (feelers
of insects)
amoeba – **amoebas** or **amoebae**
BUT **larva** – **larvae**

(xvii) For words from the Latin ending in **um**, add
either an **s** or drop the **um** and add **a** for the
plural:
memorandum – **memorandums** or **memoranda**
curriculum – **curriculums** or **curricula**
*(I prefer the **s** ending.)*

(xviii) For words from the Latin ending in **ex** or **ix**,
add either **es** or drop the **ex/ix** and add **ices**:
appendix (notes) – **appendixes** or **appendices**
index – **indexes** (e.g. alphabetical list of names)
or **indices** (technical usage)

(xix) For words from the French ending in **eau** add
either an **s** or an **x**:
beau – **beaus** or **beaux**
*(The preference is for the **s** ending.)*

Suffixes 1

(A suffix refers to word endings such as **ing**, **able**, **ed**, **en**, **ence**, **ance**, **ish**. We'll start with **ing/ed** endings first, then move on to other suffixes. It is helpful to distinguish between words with short vowels, e.g. **cop** and those with long vowels, e.g. **cope**.)

   (i) If a verb of one syllable ends in a consonant preceded by a short vowel, double the consonant before adding **ing/ed**:
     mop – mopping/mopped

  (ii) If, on the other hand, a verb of one syllable ends in a silent **e**, preceded by a long vowel, drop the **e** before adding **ing/ed**:
     mope – moping/moped

(Notice that for the verb with a short vowel (**mop**), we doubled the consonant (**mopping**), but not for the verb with the long vowel (**mope – moping**). This helps us with the spelling of other words, e.g. **hatter**, **dinner**, etc. [short vowel = double consonant], unlike **hater**, **diner**, etc. [long vowel = single consonant].)

  (iii) If the final consonant of a verb with one syllable is preceded by two vowels, then the consonant is not doubled:

    weed – weeding/weeded
BUT **wed – wedding/wedded** – See Rule (i)

(iv) If **ing/ed** is added to a verb of more than one
syllable, the final consonant is doubled only
if the **last** syllable of the word is stressed, if it
isn't, then it's not:
BEN-e-fit – benefiting/benefited
be-GIN – beginning/(began)
be-FIT – befitting/befitted
de-VEL-op – developing/developed

The consonant is, however, usually doubled
after verbs ending in **g**, **l** and (at times) **p**, i.e. in
defiance of the rule:
WOR-ship – worshipping/worshipped
MAR-vel – marvelling/marvelled
HUM-bug – humbugging/humbugged
(Sorry, but you were warned about exceptions!)

(v) If a word ends in a silent consonant, the
consonant is not doubled before adding **ing/
ed**:
crochet – crocheting/crocheted

(vi) If a word ends in a hard **c** sound, add **k**
followed by **ing/ed**:
picnic – picnicking/picnicked
panic – panicking/panicked

Suffixes 2

(This section deals with adjectives ending in **ous**.)

(i) Most nouns remain unchanged when adding **ous**:

mountain – mountainous

(ii) If a word ends in **e**, drop it before adding **ous**:

grieve – grievous

(iii) If an **e** follows a soft **g** sound, retain the **e** before adding **ous**:

advantage – advantageous

(iv) If a noun ends in **y**, replace it with **e** before adding **ous**:

beauty – beauteous

(v) If a noun ends in **f**, replace it with **v** before adding **ous**:

mischief – mischievous

(vi) To a word ending in **el**, double the **l** before adding **ous**:

marvel – marvellous

Suffixes 3

(i) Drop one **l** in **full** if added to the end of a
    word:
    care + full = careful

(ii) If a word ending in a double **l** is added to the
     beginning of a word, drop one **l**:
     skill + full = skilful

(iii) Words ending in a vowel remain unchanged if
      ly is added:
      free – freely

(iv) Words ending in **l** remain unchanged if **ly** is
     added:
     fatal – fatally

(v) If a suffix is added to a word ending in **y**,
    retain the **y** if preceded by a vowel; if not,
    change it to an **i**:
    enjoy – enjoyable
    rely – reliable
    reply – replied

(vi) If a word ends in a vowel followed by **e**, drop
     the **e** for a suffix beginning with either **a** or **e**:
     value – valuable
     plague – plagued

(vii) **-able/-ible**: The previous two points dealt with the addition of **able** (and other suffixes) to words in certain categories. Our present concern is with the difference in usage between **able** and **ible** endings. The suffix **able** is *generally* used for words that suggest being **able** to do something:

like – likable (i.e. being able to 'like')
change – changeable (i.e. being able to 'change')
appreciate – appreciable (i.e. being able to 'appreciate')
use – useable or **usable** (i.e. being able to be 'used')

Now, let's move on to **ible**. And here we can't be prescriptive. The only good news is that there are far more **able** than **ible** endings. Some commentators would have it that words to which **able** is added can, in many instances, make sense on their own, whereas those to which **ible** is added, do not: **move**, for instance, makes sense on its own, therefore add **able**, i.e. **move – moveable** (**movable** is also acceptable); **neglig**, on the other hand, does not make sense on its own, therefore add **ible**, i.e. **negligible**. As usual, though, there are exceptions, e.g. **irrit** cannot stand on its own, but is spelt **irritable**; **access** can stand on its own, but is spelt **accessible**.

What a mess! However, here are some of the more

common **ible** endings:

> **admissible, audible, compatible,**
> **comprehensible, contemptible, credible,**
> **defensible, digestible, divisible, edible,**
> **eligible, feasible, flexible, gullible, horrible,**
> **indelible, intelligible, invincible, irresistible,**
> **legible, perceptible, permissible, possible,**
> **reprehensible, responsible, sensible,**
> **susceptible, terrible, visible.**

(viii) **ery/ary**: as a general rule – there are exceptions – **nouns** end in **ery**, **adjectives** in **ary:**

stationery (noun) – writing pads, pencils, etc.

stationary (adjective) – not moving

Some exceptions: **dictionary** (noun), **estuary** (noun), **secretary** (noun). Bear in mind, though, that more words end in **ary** than in **ery.**

(ix) If a verb ends in **a**, **i**, **o**, **u** (i.e. vowels except **e**) or **y**, the word remains unchanged if a vowel suffix is added:

alibi – alibiing/alibied

tattoo – tattooing/tatooed

Prefixes

(i) Words beginning with **n** to which the prefix **un** is added; unchanged:
   necessary – unnecessary

(ii) Words beginning with **l**, **m** or **r**, to which **il**, **im** or **ir**, respectively, is added; unchanged:
   legal – illegal
   material – immaterial
   recoverable – irrecoverable

(iii) Words beginning with **s** to which the prefix **dis** is added; unchanged:
   soluble – dissoluble

(iv) Words like **proceed** and **supercede** sometimes cause confusion: it is unclear whether a single or double **e** should follow in the second syllable. The rule is straightforward: use a double **e** if preceded by the prefixes **suc**, **ex** and **pro**, but a single **e** for other prefixes:
   succeed, exceed, proceed
   BUT **recede, precede, concede**

ISE or IZE?

In most cases, either is acceptable, but stick to one or the other. Some verbs, such as **advertise**, **comprise**, **despise**, **surprise**, etc. and some nouns, such as **enterprise**, **franchise**, etc. always end in **ise**. On the other hand, certain words can only be spelt with the **z**, e.g. **size**, **prize** (reward), **seize**, etc. My preference is for **ise** as it causes fewer problems than **ize**.

ER/RE Endings

For words such as these always use the **re** ending (not **er** as in the US):

> **metre** (but **meter** for **parking-meter**, etc.),
> **kilometre, calibre, theatre, timbre** (voice, but
> **timber** for **wood**)

I Before E

After long **e** sounds, '**i** comes before **e**, except after **c**':

   ach**ie**ve but rec**ei**pt

Exceptions include: **neither**, **leisure**, **heist**, **weird**

C and S

Use **c** for the noun and **s** for the verb in these cases:

> **practice** (N) – **practise** (V)
> **advice** (N) – **advise** (V)
> **licence** (N) – **license** (V)
> **prophecy** (N) – **prophesy** (V)
> **device** (N) – **devise** (V)

Alternative Spellings

Some words can be spelt (spelled) in one of two ways. It is not important which option you choose; what is important, though, is that usage should be consistent. Here are some more examples: **leant/leaned**, **learnt/learned**, **focused/focussed**, **focusing/focussing**, etc. Then there's the word **bus**: the spelling of its plural noun form is **buses**; however, as a verb, either one or two **s's** may be used, i.e. **buses/busses**, **bused/bussed**, **busing/bussing**. Thus, as a noun: **Six of the buses were late this morning**; *BUT* as a verb: **He buses (or busses) to work every day**, *AND* **He bused or bussed ...** etc. The word **gas** is slightly different. As a noun, its plural is **gases**; as a verb, there is a problem: some dictionaries allow only **gases**, others **gasses**, but all are agreed that only **gassed** and **gassing** are acceptable. Thus, as a noun: **It contains a mixture of gases**, *AND* as a verb, some (e.g. *Oxford*) accept only: **He gases vermin**, while others (e.g. *Chambers*) accept only: **He gasses vermin**. It's enough to give anyone nightmares! The answer? Use a double **s** for all the verbs!

Terrible Twos

The 'terrible twos' are words with the same – or almost the same – pronunciation, but with a different spelling and meaning. There are also a number of equally terrible threes, with the same characteristics. All one can hope to do is to learn the distinction between then. Here are some examples:

altar – alter,
beat – beet,
boarder – border,
born – borne – bourn – bourne (!),
canvas – canvass,
choir – quire,
council – counsel,
currant – current,
dependant – dependent,
dew – due,
dual – duel,
fair – fare,
flair – flare,
grate – great,
hear – here,
heard – herd,
kneed – need,
knew – new,
knight – night,
knit – nit,
knot – not,
know – no,
made – maid,

main – mane,
pare – pair – pear,
principal – principle,
rain – reign – rein,
right – rite – write,
scene – seen,
scent – sent,
sew – sow,
sight – site,
soar – sore,
their – there,
vale – veil,
vane – vein,
waist – waste,
ware – wear – where,
weak – week,
weather – wether – whether,
whole – hole,
wreak – reek.

(See also the section on Correct Usage.)

Syllabification

There are times when dividing words into their syllables is a useful aid to correct – or nearly correct! – spelling. Although, as we have seen, English is not really a phonetic language, this exercise is often, nevertheless, pretty effective. It is always a good idea, where possible, to begin each syllable with a consonant. Let's try a few:

**syl-la-bi-fi-ca-tion, ac-com-mo-da-tion,
con-tem-po-ra-ry, bur-gun-dy,
ce-me-te-ry, ne-ces-sa-ry, wool-len,
ve-te-ri-na-ry**, and so on.

This is not, of course, possible in all cases, and would certainly not be helpful in the following instances:

phthisis (tie-sis) – this because, as one of my teachers explained many years ago 'The p is silent, as in swimming';

awry – syllabification would probably have given us a spelling such as **arye**!

One of the longest words in the English language is **floccinaucinihilipilification** (29 letters), which dates back to the 18th Century. Would syllabification have allowed us to arrive at the correct spelling? I doubt it! By the way, this means, facetiously, 'setting at little or no value'.

In 1964, in the film, *Mary Poppins*, it was trumped by an even longer word, which now appears in most dictionaries, namely, **su-per-ca-li-fra-gi-lis-tic-ex-pi-a-li-do-ci-ous** (34 letters), meaning, 'absolutely stunningly fantastic'. Notice how, in this case, the word responded to syllabification.

So, there we have it, though I'm not, of course, advocating that these rules should be learnt by heart – I, certainly, can't remember them all. On the other hand, they are useful points of reference, and account for the correct spelling of literally thousands of words. (If you don't believe me – start counting!) And for those inclined to ignore them, what can be easier than to fall back on the most important rule of all: *When in doubt, consult a dictionary*. That's all right, then, isn't it – or should that be alright? None the less – or is it nonetheless – English spelling remains a minefield (mine-field?/mine field?), doesn't it?

What better way to end than with this delightfully witty poem by Dutch writer, Dr Gerald Nolst Trenite (1870–1946) that (which? – damn, I still never know which is right!) says all there is to be said about the unpredictability of English pronunciation and, albeit obliquely, the negative impact this has had on English spelling.

The Chaos

Dearest creature in creation,
Study English pronunciation.
I will teach you in my verse
Sounds like corpse, corps, horse, and worse.
I will keep you, Suzy, busy,
Make your head with heat grow dizzy.
Tear in eye, your dress will tear.
So shall I! Oh, hear my prayer.

Just compare heart, beard, and heard,
Dies and diet, lord and word,
Sword and sward, retain and Britain.
(Mind the latter, how it's written.)
Now I surely will not plague you
With such words as plaque and ague.
But be careful how you speak:
Say break and steak, but bleak and streak;
Cloven, oven, how and low,
Script, receipt, show, poem, and toe.

Hear me say, devoid of trickery,
Daughter, laughter, and Terpsichore,
Typhoid, measles, topsails, aisles,
Exiles, similes, and reviles;

Scholar, vicar, and cigar,
Solar, mica, war and far;
One, anemone, Balmoral,
Kitchen, lichen, laundry, laurel;
Gertrude, German, wind and mind,
Scene, Melpomene, mankind.

Billet does not rhyme with ballet,
Bouquet, wallet, mallet, chalet.
Blood and flood are not like food,
Nor is mould like should and would.
Viscous, viscount, load and broad,
Toward, to forward, to reward.
And your pronunciation's OK
When you correctly say croquet,
Rounded, wounded, grieve and sleeve,
Friend and fiend, alive and live.

Ivy, privy, famous; clamour
And enamour rhyme with hammer.
River, rival, tomb, bomb, comb,
Doll and roll and some and home.
Stranger does not rhyme with anger,
Neither does devour with clangour.
Souls but foul, haunt but aunt,
Font, front, wont, want, grand, and grant,
Shoes, goes, does. Now first say finger,
And then singer, ginger, linger,

Real, zeal, mauve, gauze, gouge and gauge,
Marriage, foliage, mirage, and age.

Query does not rhyme with very,
Nor does fury sound like bury.
Dost, lost, post and doth, cloth, loth.
Job, nob, bosom, transom, oath.
Though the differences seem little,
We say actual but victual.
Refer does not rhyme with deafer.
Foeffer does, and zephyr, heifer.
Mint, pint, senate and sedate;
Dull, bull, and George ate late.
Scenic, Arabic, Pacific,
Science, conscience, scientific.

Liberty, library, heave and heaven,
Rachel, ache, moustache, eleven.
We say hallowed, but allowed,
People, leopard, towed, but vowed.
Mark the differences, moreover,
Between mover, cover, clover;
Leeches, breeches, wise, precise,
Chalice, but police and lice;
Camel, constable, unstable,
Principle, disciple, label.

Petal, panel, and canal,
Wait, surprise, plait, promise, pal.

Worm and storm, chaise, chaos, chair,
Senator, spectator, mayor.
Tour, but our and succour, four.
Gas, alas, and Arkansas.
Sea, idea, Korea, area,
Psalm, Maria, but malaria.
Youth, south, southern, cleanse and clean.
Doctrine, turpentine, marine.

Compare alien with Italian,
Dandelion and battalion.
Sally with ally, yea, ye,
Eye, I, ay, aye, whey, and key.
Say aver, but ever, fever,
Neither, leisure, skein, deceiver.
Heron, granary, canary.
Crevice and device and aerie.

Face, but preface, not efface.
Phlegm, phlegmatic, ass, glass, bass.
Large, but target, gin, give, verging,
Ought, out, joust and scour, scourging.
Ear, but earn and wear and tear
Do not rhyme with here but ere.
Seven is right, but so is even,
Hyphen, roughen, nephew Stephen,
Monkey, donkey, Turk and jerk,
Ask, grasp, wasp, and cork and work.

Pronunciation – think of Psyche!
Is a paling stout and spikey?
Won't it make you lose your wits,
Writing groats and saying grits?
It's a dark abyss or tunnel:
Strewn with stones, stowed, solace,
   gunwale,
Islington and Isle of Wight,
Housewife, verdict and indict.

Finally, which rhymes with enough –
Though, through, plough, or dough, or
   cough?
Hiccough has the sound of cup.
My advice is just give up!

Bibliography

BRANFORD, JEAN. 1980. *A Dictionary of South African English*. Oxford University Press. Cape Town.

Cambridge English Pronouncing Dictionary. 2003. Cambridge University Press.

Chambers 21st Century Dictionary. 1996. Chambers. Edinburgh.

CRYSTAL, DAVID. 1990. *The English Language*. Penguin Books.

FOWLER, H W. 1958. *Modern English Usage*. Oxford University Press.

FOWLER, H W and FOWLER, F G. 1938. *The King's English*. Oxford at the Clarendon Press.

GOWERS, Sir ERNEST. 1955. *The Complete Plain Words*. London. Her Majesty's Stationery Office.

Odhams Dictionary of the English Language. Odhams Press Limited. London.

Oxford Advanced Learner's Dictionary. 1992. Oxford

University Press.

PARTRIDGE, ERIC. 1974. *Usage & Abusage*. Penguin Books in association with Hamish Hamilton.

Quickfix. 1993. Edward Arnold Australia.

South African Concise Oxford Dictionary. 2002. Oxford University Press.

Guidelines on Terms and Punctuation. 1997. The English Academy of Southern Africa.

The Oxford Dictionary for Writers and Editors. 1981. Clarendon Press. Oxford.

The Shorter Oxford English Dictionary on Historical Principles. 1980. Clarendon Press. Oxford.

TREBLE, H A and VALLINS, G H. 1954. *An A.B.C. of English Usage*. Oxford at the Clarendon Press.

WEBB, ROBERT A. 1978. *The Washington Post Deskbook on Style*. McGraw-Hill Book Company.

Acknowledgements

A number of quotations are taken from J M and
M J Cohen's *A Dictionary of Modern Quotations*, 1973,
Penguin Books and from the Oxford University Press's
Dictionary of Quotations, Second Edition, 1985, while
other extracts are as attributed. I'm also indebted to
The Spectator of 11 March 2006 for the information
about Ronnie Barker and, as a matter of 'Netiquette',
to yourdictionary.com (http://www.yourdictionary.
com/library/tough.html) for first drawing my attention
to the poem – also on multiple sites – by Dr Gerald
Nolst Trenite. My thanks to Joel Alswang, formerly
Superintendent of Education, for his comments and
suggestions, and to Terry Morris, MD of Pan Macmillan
South Africa, whose idea it all was.

Index